SO YOU THINK YOU'RE A
KANSAS CITY ROYALS
FAN?

STARS, STATS, RECORDS, AND MEMORIES FOR TRUE DIEHARDS

CURT NELSON

SPORTS
PUBLISHING

To my parents Bob and Ellen, my brothers Erik and Mitch, and all my family and friends—thanks for allowing me to be me, and loving me anyway. And to my nephew Nicklaus, that you will always find the same support from all of us who love you.

Contents

Intro–Pregame   *vii*

Early Innings: Rookie Level   1

Middle Innings: Veteran Level   47

Late Innings: All-Star Level   91

Extra Innings: Hall of Fame Level   143

Intro–Pregame

"How long have you been with the Royals?" The question is one I've been asked many times over many years, and I always respond the same way. The query is actually a trick question for me, because there are two ways to go about the answer. I can say how long I've worked for the ballclub, since the start of the 1999 season. But my heartfelt answer is to say I've been with the Royals from the very start.

Ewing and Muriel Kauffman were awarded ownership of Kansas City's American League expansion franchise on January 11, 1968. Just a little over a month later in Tulsa, Oklahoma, on February 16, 1968, my parents Bob and Ellen Nelson welcomed me into the world. I like to think the Royals and I both got lucky starts together: the ballclub born in Kansas City with Mr. and Mrs. K at its side; me in Tulsa with my mom and dad at mine.

So, if you want to know how old the Royals are, you can take a look at me. We are the same age, although the ballclub is in much better physical shape—and it never has to carve out time to try to trim down with miles run on a treadmill. We are nearing a half-century together now, and the Royals have been part of my life from the get-go. Like so many others, I can link the different times of my life—both my triumphs and disappointments—with my connection to the Royals (in both their triumphs and disappointments). I'm biased and a bit romantic when it comes to baseball and its power to generate special moments that can create collectively shared lifelong memories. But I know the game has that power because I've had the thrill of experiencing those moments as a fan; and I've also had the privilege of living them as a member of the Royals organization.

Any time I hear Fred White's radio call of George Brett's home run against Goose Gossage in Game 3 of the 1980 American League Championship Series, I'm transported back to being my 12-year-old self and the thrill of that moment. That very same 12-year-old is still crying about our loss to the Phillies in the 1980 World Series, especially the heartbreaking ending of Game 5 at Royals Stadium. My brothers and I can still vividly remember watching Dane Iorg's pinch hit fall in Game 6 of the 1985 World Series and watching breathlessly as Jim Sundberg slid across home plate with the series-tying run. That series ended the way we wanted it to, and it remains a touchstone for a generation of Royals fans.

Those are just a few of the moments from the early years of Royals history that stay with me in great detail all these years later. I think of them as *my* Royals moments; perhaps you share them with me. If so, I hope you'll enjoy learning more about them—or being reminded of them—here. This book is for you, the lifelong Royals fan, because it was written by one of you (namely me).

Having said that, one of my greatest thrills from 2014 and 2015 was watching those two seasons unfold in the eyes of a whole new generation of Royals fans. Now those fans can better understand the older generation's reverence for earlier Royals triumphs. Salvador Perez's game-winning hit in the 2014 American League Wild Card Game—you'll always remember where you were when it happened. Eric Hosmer's mad dash for home in Game 5 of the 2015 World Series took your breath away and it still will when you are a couple of decades older—I can assure you of that. Those and so many more are now *your* moments, and I'm so glad to share them with you.

This book is not intended as a complete history of the Royals franchise. There are many stories, moments, and people not covered here, or at least not in deep detail—there simply is not enough space to cover it all. However, I did want this book to help provide a baseline of knowledge about the organization's history that all Royals fans should know if they don't already—and hopefully provide a little more detail for some stories you may have thought you already knew. You might even be able to win a few bar bets, with the caveats that I do not condone you actually making wagers—and no bellying up to the bar unless you are 21 years of age or older anyway.

So You Think You're a Kansas City Royals Fan? isn't meant to be a challenge to your Royals fandom as much as it is an open invitation to know more about the baseball team you and I have come to love: all of that along with a mixture of oddities, peculiarities, interesting connections, and some outright strange (but true) facts from the history of Royals baseball so far.

When my parents brought me to Royals Stadium throughout my childhood, I would tell them I wanted to work there someday. I learned early, probably as far back as tee-ball, that my course to the big leagues was not going to be on the field. And I was right.

But with their support, the encouragement of many others along the way, and the opportunities provided by my favorite team, here I am living my big-league dream. I'm fortunate to have been given the chance to make my fervent avocation an actual career-making vocation. If you are reading this then I know we probably share the former; and I hope this book illustrates my devotion and thankfulness for the latter.

Go Royals!

ROOKIE LEVEL

1. Where did the name "Royals" come from? *Answer on page 3.*

2. What year did Royals Stadium open? *Answer on page 7.*

3. What is the significance of the numbers 20, 10, and 5 on the Royals Hall of Fame building at Kauffman Stadium? *Answer on page 10.*

4. Why are the Royals' primary colors blue and white? *Answer on page 11.*

5. Who is the Royals' mascot? *Answer on page 12.*

6. Who founded the Royals? *Answer on page 13.*

7. How many times have the Royals played in the World Series? *Answer on page 16.*

8. Which Royals have won American League Rookie of the Year honors (through 2016)? *Answer on page 17.*

9. Who were the first inductees into the Royals Hall of Fame? *Answer on page 20.*

10. Which manager has won the most games in Royals history? *Answer on page 22.*

11. Why are fountains a key feature of Kauffman Stadium? *Answer on page 23.*

12. In what season did the Royals debut their first powder blue uniforms? *Answer on page 25.*

13. Who is the youngest player to ever appear for the Royals? *Answer on page 26.*

14. Who scored the first run in Royals history? *Answer on page 27.*

15. In what season did Kauffman Stadium change from artificial turf to natural grass? *Answer on page 29.*

16. How many hits did George Brett have in his Hall of Fame career? *Answer on page 29.*

17. What is the Royals record for most team wins in a single season? *Answer on page 30.*

18. Which two Royals players jumped into the Royals Stadium fountains after the Royals clinched their first-ever division title? *Answer on page 31.*

19. What two Royals players have won Major League Baseball All-Star Game Most Valuable Player honors? *Answer on page 32.*

20. Where is the Royals Triple-A minor-league affiliate? *Answer on page 35.*

21. Which Royals player drove in the winning runs in Game 6 of the 1985 World Series? *Answer on page 36.*

22. Which Royals player drove in the go-ahead run in the clinching Game 5 of the 2015 World Series? *Answer on page 39.*

23. When was Royals Stadium officially renamed Kauffman Stadium? *Answer on page 40.*

24. How many Rawlings Gold Gloves did Royals Hall of Famer Frank White win in his career? *Answer on page 42.*

25. How many All-Star Games have the Royals hosted? *Answer on page 43.*

ROOKIE LEVEL — ANSWERS

1. The origin of a team name is always an important part of the history of a franchise and its connection to the city it calls home. Where did the name "Royals" come from and how is it tied specifically to Kansas City? Believe it or not, it goes all the way back to 1899—a full seven decades before the Kansas City Royals ever took the field.

Shortly after Ewing and Muriel Kauffman were awarded the American League expansion franchise on January 11, 1968, they ceded the naming of the team to Kansas City baseball fans through a "Name the Team" contest in cooperation with the *Kansas City Star* newspaper. The suggestions came rolling in with more than 17,000 entries submitted showing a wide range of ideas. Some were odes to previous Kansas City baseball teams, others allusions to the area being the geographic heartland of the country, and some were downright silly references to Kauffman himself and his success in the pharmaceutical industry. The proposed names included Blues, Monarchs, Mules, Steers, Hearts, Stars, MoKans, Caseys, Scouts, Kauffers, and Capsules.

Although Kauffman was thought to be partial to Kings, Stars, and Eagles, the most often submitted name by fans was Royals, and Kauffman needed very little convincing, declaring, "The name Kansas City Royals definitely is a winner." With that unabashed endorsement, the team name was chosen and an official announcement was made on March 21, 1968.

But you could still rightly ask—why Royals? How is the name a natural extension of the city and its history?

There had been other professional teams that carried the Royals name. The Montreal Royals were a minor-league baseball team of note for decades. They even have a special place in baseball history shared with Kansas City. National Baseball Hall of Famer Jackie Robinson made his professional baseball debut with the Kansas City Monarchs in 1945 before he was signed by the Brooklyn Dodgers and broke Major League Baseball's unwritten, but unmistakable color barrier in 1947. In the season between his 1945 professional debut with the Monarchs and his historic debut with the Dodgers in 1947, Robinson broke the color barrier in the Triple-A International League playing for the 1946 Montreal Royals, then the top minor-league affiliate of the Brooklyn Dodgers.

So the question often arises, did the Royals name have any connection to minor-league baseball's famed Montreal Royals?

Not at all.

There were the Rochester Royals who won the 1951 NBA championship over the New York Knicks. Those Royals later moved to Cincinnati in 1957, and as fate would have it, to Kansas City in 1972. Their move to Kansas City came after the baseball Royals had started play in 1969, which spurred that franchise to change its name to the Kings. The Kings left Kansas City in 1985 for Sacramento, California, where they still play today.

Thus, others sometimes ask, did the Royals name have any connection to the NBA's Rochester/Cincinnati Royals?

None whatsoever.

Finally, Kansas City was the site of the founding of the Negro National League in 1920 and was the home of one of the

most famous and consequential teams in Negro League Baseball history—and baseball history in general. The Kansas City
Monarchs won the first Negro World Series in 1924, defeating
the Eastern Colored League champion Hilldale Club five games
to four. There are more Monarchs players in the National Baseball Hall of Fame than any other club from the Negro Leagues.
Greats from Satchel Paige to Hilton Smith, Bullet Joe Rogan to
Ernie Banks, and of course Jackie Robinson himself wore the
Monarchs uniform in Kansas City.

Considering the prestige of those who played for them,
was the Royals name an homage to the legacy of the Kansas
City Monarchs*? Nope, at least not directly.

*The origin of the Monarchs name is not easily found in history
or lore—it might have had some of the same origins as the Kansas
City Royals, but that's another story.

No, the name Royals has a much clearer and direct tie to
an enduring Kansas City cultural institution.

The name Royals was submitted on 547 entries, the most
of any in the "Name the Team" contest. Kauffman and the board
of the new ballclub selected one of those entries as the contest
winner. The submission they choose came from Overland Park,
Kansas, resident Sanford Porte. His entry was chosen for its
"neatness" and "logical reasoning." Here is part of what he wrote:

"Kansas City's new baseball team should be called the
Royals because of Missouri's billion-dollar livestock income,
Kansas City's position as the nation's leading stocker and feeder
market and the nationally known American Royal parade and
pageant."

That's right. The Royals name has its origins in one of Kansas City's longest-running traditions known as "The American
Royal," or more colloquially "The Royal," which dates back to

Royals founder Ewing Kauffman, general manager Cedric Tallis, and "Name the Team" contest winner Sanford Porte at the press conference announcing "Royals" as the name for Kansas City's American League expansion franchise (March 21, 1968). Porte's entry was selected as the winner in the "Name the Team" contest held by the *Kansas City Star* to choose the name of Kansas City's new expansion baseball team.

1899. The American Royal started as the National Hereford Show in 1899, which was the first nationwide event for the exposition and sale of pure-bred cattle. The inaugural year the event drew 55,000 people and helped establish a tradition that continues today.

The American Royal grew to include one of the country's most important horse shows in 1905 and was a significant economic force in helping Kansas City become a vital agricultural hub. Kansas City's economy has become much more diversified, and the "Cowtown" image is largely history now—but it remains an important and fundamental part of the overall history of both the city and the country.

The American Royal lives on today, and perhaps its most well-known element now is the barbecue competition introduced in 1980, the year of the Royals' first American League pennant. Though no single state, city, or locale can claim to have invented barbecue, Kansas City will proudly stake a claim on having perfected the craft. With more barbecue restaurants per capita than any other city, Kansas City's barbecue tradition stacks up to anywhere in the country. If you've never had burnt ends, then you need to go to Kansas City and give them a try—you can thank us later (and if you enjoy barbecue at all you will).

Through the American Royal, the Royals name has a deep connection to Kansas City's cultural history. And now the American Royal has a deep connection to the Kansas City culinary tradition of barbecue. Royals baseball and barbecue— there is nothing more Kansas City than that.

Did You Know?—When Casey Coleman made his Royals debut on May 16, 2014, he became the first "Casey"—first or last name (any spelling)— to appear as a member of the "KC" Royals.

2. Royals Stadium made its debut on April 10, 1973 on a cold and brisk Kansas City night with the gametime temperature recorded at 39 degrees—and it only got chillier over the course of the two hour, 25-minute contest against the Texas Rangers. In fact, that very morning there had been scattered snow flurries in the area, so the ballpark's grand opening almost literally broke the ice on a new era for Kansas City baseball.

Royals Stadium during pregame ceremonies on Opening Night before the Royals hosted the Texas Rangers for the ballpark's debut game (April 10, 1973).

Although Royals Stadium hosted its first game in 1973, the project to build a new ballpark in Kansas City predated the birth of the Royals by several years. One of the key disputes between the Kansas City Athletics and the city had centered on the rent costs of Municipal Stadium and the desire for a new more modern and up-to-date facility. The friction was one factor in Athletics owner Charlie Finley's ongoing battles that eventually resulted in him moving his franchise to Oakland after the 1967 season—but with Finley there was always a tangled web of reasons, motivations, and slights (perceived or real).

The bond issue that funded a new ballpark in Kansas City was actually passed on June 27, 1967. On that particular Tuesday, the Athletics were still the Kansas City Athletics, and the Kansas City Royals were not yet a thing or even a thought.

Of course that would quickly change just months later. First, Finley was finally allowed to move his team—which he had seemingly been trying to accomplish for several years—with the official backing of an affirmative vote by his fellow American League owners on October 18, 1967. Then at that same owners meeting Kansas City was promised an expansion franchise, although with an ill-defined timetable set "as soon as practical, not later than 1971." With the stadium project already in place, sooner was certainly better for Kansas City.

The approved bond issue, along with the extra heft of US senator Stuart Symington (D-MO), worked in the favor of Kansas City representatives in their efforts to speed the expansion timeline. The following day American League owners revised their commitment to say Kansas City would receive an expansion franchise to begin play in the 1969 season. And with that, the birth of the Kansas City Royals was set in motion.

So the 1973 debut of Royals Stadium was the conclusion of a project that had started before the inception of the Kansas City Royals, the Royals history version of the causality conundrum, "what came first, the chicken or the egg?"

Did You Know?—*When it opened, Royals Stadium was the first all artificial turf playing field in American League history. Comiskey Park had an artificial turf infield with a natural grass outfield from 1969 to 1975.*

3. The most simple and straightforward answer is that those are the first three jersey numbers retired by the Kansas City Royals. However, the symmetry of their order of display is different from the chronology of their actual retirement.

The first number retired was Dick Howser's number 10 on July 3, 1987. Howser led the Royals to three postseason appearances in just over five years as manager from 1981 through 1986—including the Royals first world championship in 1985. Unfortunately, the former Royals manager received the honor posthumously as he had passed away just weeks earlier on June 17, 1987 at the age of 51 following a battle with brain cancer. Howser was also inducted that night as the fifth member of the Royals Hall of Fame.

The ceremony took place between games of a doubleheader at Royals Stadium against the Toronto Blue Jays. The Royals pounded out a dozen hits including three-hit games from both Willie Wilson and Danny Tartabull, powering them to a 6–4 win in Game 1. Frank White's one-out solo homer in the bottom of the second put the Royals in front in Game 2. But the Blue Jays led 4–3 going into the bottom of the ninth, when Juan Beniquez started a one-out rally with a single. Then pinch-runner Willie Wilson stole second, and with two outs, Tom Henke intentionally walked George Brett—but then walked Danny Tartabull to load the bases. Wilson scored the tying run on a wild pitch and an RBI single by Frank White scored Brett for a 5–4 walkoff win in Game 2. The sweep on Dick Howser

Night fittingly put the Royals into a first-place tie in the American League Western Division (with the Twins).

The second number retired by the Royals was George Brett's number 5 on May 14, 1994. During pregame ceremonies that evening, George Brett was inducted as the 12th member of the Royals Hall of Fame. Brett had played his final game at the conclusion of the 1993 season—but as the greatest player in franchise history, there was no waiting period necessary to celebrate the obvious. Part of the celebration included the official retiring of Brett's iconic number 5. Only the required five-year waiting period stood between Brett and his eventual place in the National Baseball Hall of Fame—he would be part of the Cooperstown Class of 1999.

The third number retired by the Royals was hometown hero Frank White's number 20 on July 2, 1995. Although White was born in Greenville, Mississippi, he was Kansas City through and through. The White family moved to Kansas City when Frank was three years old, and he eventually attended Lincoln High School, which was located right next to Municipal Stadium. Frank was a graduate of the innovative Royals Baseball Academy that provided him both the unique opportunity and challenge of playing for his hometown team. He earned his legend on the playing field, and the loyalty of fans was even stronger because he was one of Kansas City's very own.

Did You Know?—Major League Baseball retired number 42 across the game in honor of Jackie Robinson in 1997. The last player to wear number 42 for the Royals was outfielder Tom Goodwin (1995–1997).

4. Blue and white make perfect sense as colors for a team called the Royals, but they were not the only fitting options available. There are perfectly good reasons the colors of red or gold would have been appropriate. But in Kansas City those were already the colors of football season. And no one would have batted an eye if purple—the color of royalty—had been chosen.

Yet blue is a hue that also hits the mark—and royal blue is nearly perfect. So the Royals went with blue, but there was another early indicator that might have given away the direction the Kansas City expansion team would take, at least in regard to the franchise's chosen colors.

The American League awarded the expansion club to Ewing Kauffman and his wife Muriel on January 11, 1968. Although the team name had not yet been chosen, a little research might have given a clue as to what the team colors would later become. All you needed to do was look to the horse track.

The Kauffmans were already in the sports business in a smaller fashion with racehorses. Perhaps the only overlap between their two sporting endeavors turned out to be the colors of blue and white. The silks worn by horses owned by the Kauffmans were already blue and white—there was no real need to make a change.

After the name Royals was selected, and the colors of blue and white were chosen, Mr. Kauffman joked he could simply make one of his horses that wasn't winning at the track available to be the baseball team's mascot. The mascot idea had no legs, but the colors have certainly stood the test of time.

5. Sluggerrr.

Well, if a horse wouldn't work as a mascot—then what would? The mascot question lingered for almost two decades after the founding of the Royals. The answer wouldn't reveal itself until 1996.

The Royals made an announcement during the offseason after the 1995 season that the 1996 home opener would include the addition of a first-ever mascot. And much like the naming of the team back in 1968, the naming of the new mascot would be left to Royals fans. But what would the mascot be?

The mascot-naming contest began in early 1996 and was co-sponsored by the Royals and the *Kansas City Star*. Although the details of the mascot weren't given, a clawed paw and tail appeared in the print advertisements. The clues clearly hinted at a royal creature—perhaps the proverbial king of the jungle. And so it turned out to be on Opening Day.

The Royals debuted their very regal lion named Sluggerrr during pregame ceremonies, then roared out to a walkoff win, of course. The Royals trailed 4–3 entering the bottom of the ninth inning when David Howard led off with a single and stole second. He moved to third on a passed ball and scored the tying run on a one-out RBI double by Mike Macfarlane.

Tom Goodwin then reached base leading off the bottom of the 12th inning on an error charged to shortstop John Valentin. With one out Goodwin stole second; with two outs he stole third; then he scored the winning run on an RBI single by Patrick Lennon. It was the one and only RBI for Lennon as a member of the Royals, but he made it count with a walkoff victory in the home opener. The Royals defeated Boston 5–4 in 12 innings at Kauffman Stadium—making Sluggerrr a winner from the very start.

6. The Royals were founded by Ewing Marion Kauffman and his wife Muriel. They were chosen by the American League as owners of the Kansas City expansion franchise—a decision that was made official on January 11, 1968. But the story of how and why goes back much further and has many more layers.

So You Think You're a Kansas City Royals Fan?

The Royals' story is truly a tale of and about Kansas City. The origins of the franchise started from civic reaction to losing a team that had not originally been Kansas City born. The lack of local roots was one reason many believed the Athletics' stay in Kansas City turned out to be a temporary stop on their cross-country migration from east (Philadelphia) to west (Oakland).

Muriel and Ewing Kauffman, along with Royal Lancer Earl Smith, celebrate the 6,441 season tickets sold for the 1969 inaugural season—the most season tickets sold for any American League team.

When Kansas City was promised a new franchise in October of 1967, civic leaders went to work to find an owner who would be committed to both baseball and Kansas City. They found the perfect match of man and mission in Ewing Kauffman.

Born in Garden City, Missouri, Ewing Kauffman's family moved to Kansas City when he was eight years old and he called it home the rest of his life. His common touch was instilled by his parents, John and Effie Mae. From his father he inherited a tenacity of spirit and a curiosity for numbers, while his mother imparted a thirst for knowledge, a genuine sense of self-worth, and a deep respect for others.

After the attack on Pearl Harbor in 1941, Kauffman enlisted in the Navy, where his skill with numbers won praise from superiors and card games from shipmates who nicknamed him "Lucky." When Kauffman returned home, he found work in pharmaceutical sales. A natural, he quickly out-earned the company president, which resulted in his territory being reduced. Instead Kauffman forged his own path and founded Marion Laboratories in 1950—partially with savings from his Navy service card winnings.

To avoid looking like a one-man operation, Kauffman used his middle name Marion for the company he started in the basement of his home in 1950. Marion Laboratories posted first-year sales of $39,000 with a $1,000 net profit. By 1964, the company had profits of $130,000. By the time the company merged with Merrell Dow in 1989, the global pharmaceutical leader had 3,400 associates and nearly $1 billion in sales.

Kauffman never viewed Marion's success as his alone; he believed in sharing the rewards with the associates who made his vision a reality. Similarly, he sought to give back to the community, and that is where his baseball life began. Muriel convinced her husband that baseball could be an important outlet outside of Marion Labs. He believed baseball was an important part of the city's economy and identity.

Ewing Kauffman was a civic-minded, visionary leader who championed innovation in everything he did. But it was his love for his hometown that drove him to help bring baseball back to Kansas City—with a strong assist from his wife Muriel. Together in 1968 they made a commitment to keep baseball in Kansas City and bring home a championship—and they delivered on both promises.

7. Four.

Entering the 2017 season, the Royals had reached the World Series four times—1980, 1985, 2014, and 2015. The four World Series appearances for the Royals are the most by any American League expansion franchise and second only to the New York Mets for most by any major-league expansion club.

The Royals were the first American League expansion franchise to reach the World Series, but it didn't come in their first opportunity, or their second, or their third. After losing to the New York Yankees in the playoffs in 1976, 1977, and 1978, the fourth time was the charm. The 1980 season was a culmination of sorts for the Royals in capturing the franchise's first American League Championship and delivering a World Series to Kansas City for the first time.

The next appearance came five years later, and until recently was the most celebrated. The second chance opportunity was exactly what Royals fans had always longed for—a world championship; and even better their first climb to the top of the baseball world came against the cross-state St. Louis Cardinals. With two World Series appearances over the course of six seasons, it felt as if reaching the Fall Classic would be something that Royals fans could become accustomed to. They certainly hoped so, but it wouldn't work out that way.

Royals fans would have to wait nearly three full decades until the thrilling 2014 season for their team to reach the Fall Classic again. Unlike their first appearance in 1980, the 2014 Royals reached the World Series seemingly out of the blue, flowing from the excitement of their first playoff berth in 29 years. Similar to their first appearance in 1980, the 2014 trip to the Fall Classic was exhilarating but ended frustratingly short of the ultimate goal.

Loyalty paid off for Royals fans in countless ways with the club's fourth World Series appearance in 2015. After the Royals ended a 29-year drought, the club gave itself another chance at a title the very next year with a second consecutive American League pennant. And where 2014 came up just short, the 2015 Royals closed the deal and brought Kansas City its second summit at the top of the baseball world.

8. Lou Piniella, Bob Hamelin, Carlos Beltran, and Angel Berroa.

Through the 2016 season, four Royals players have won American League Rookie of the Year honors.

The first American League Rookie of the Year for the Royals was the man of many firsts in club history—outfielder Lou Piniella. He was the breakout star of the Royals' inaugural season after being acquired a week before that first campaign began from their fellow expansion club, the Seattle Pilots. The Royals sent pitcher John Gelnar and outfielder Steve Whitaker to Seattle in one of the better trades in franchise history.

He led the Royals in hitting with a .282 batting average and won the 1969 award, finishing in front of pitcher Mike Nagy, who won 12 games for the Red Sox.

The next Royals Rookie of the Year was Bob Hamelin after the strike-shortened 1994 season, when he finished in

Outfielder Lou Piniella won the 1969 American League Rookie of the Year Award for the expansion Royals in their inaugural season. He played for the Royals from 1969 to 1973.

front of Cleveland Indians outfielder Manny Ramirez. He led the Royals in home runs, RBIs, total bases, walks, slugging percentage, and on-base percentage. Hamelin's 24 home runs bested the then Royals rookie record of 22 set by Bo Jackson in 1987. Like Piniella, Hamelin hit .282 during his rookie campaign. He led American League rookies in games, at-bats, runs, hits, doubles, home runs, RBIs, and walks.

The third American League Rookie of the Year for the Royals had the greatest freshman year in club history. Royals outfielder Carlos Beltran hit .293 with 112 runs scored, 22 home runs, and 108 RBIs to run away with Rookie of the Year honors. Beltran was a near-unanimous winner, garnering 26 of the 28 Baseball Writers Association of America votes and easily outdistancing pitcher Freddy Garcia, who won 17 games for the Mariners.

Beltran was the first American League rookie to post 100 or more RBIs since Mark McGwire in 1987. He was only the seventh rookie in baseball history with 100 or more runs scored and 100 or more RBIs—the first since Fred Lynn in 1975. He also was just the third Royals player in history to post a season of 20 or more home runs and stolen bases, joining both Amos Otis and Bo Jackson.

Angel Berroa became the fourth Royals player voted the American League's Rookie of the Year. Berroa won the award after the 2003 season in which he hit .287 with 17 home runs and 73 RBIs, barely edging Yankees outfielder Hideki Matsui for the honors—it was the closest margin since 1979.

The history of Royals' Rookies of the Year shows that the award is no guarantee of future greatness—sometimes it is the start of something big, and sometimes the first year is the best one of a player's career. Bob Hamelin and Angel Berroa had outstanding first seasons, but then never really matched that performance again. Piniella went on to have a long career including an All-Star appearance with the Royals in 1972 and an even more decorated career as a major-league manager. The first year for Beltran was the launching pad for one of the better careers of his era, one that may make him a candidate for the National Baseball Hall of Fame in Cooperstown.

9. Amos Otis and Steve Busby were the first two inductees into the Royals Hall of Fame on June 7, 1986. The Royals Hall of Fame was established in 1986 to celebrate the history of the franchise that was then coming off its first-ever World Series win.

At the time Royals general manager John Schuerholz said: "When this organization was formed in 1969, it was formed with an idea and with a goal that focused on success. We felt as an organization we had grown in stature enough that the time had come to establish the Royals Hall of Fame. The championships we've won, the awards we've received as a team and as individual players brings us to the point that we think it is absolutely legitimate to have a hall of fame."

And the club could not have had two better representatives of their success to first bestow the organization's top honor upon. Busby was a two-time All-Star and the first pitcher in major-league history to throw no-hitters in each of his first two seasons. From 1973 to 1975, Busby averaged nearly 19 wins, 260+ innings pitched, and 177 strikeouts per season. Otis was a five-time All-Star, three-time Rawlings Gold Glove winner and was named Royals Player of the Year three times.

The first two Royals Hall of Fame plaques read:

Amos Otis
Outfielder 1970–1983
Inducted 1986

A complete player and gifted performer, Otis excelled in every facet of the game. He was named Royals Player of the Year three times and was selected to five All-Star teams. Known as one of his era's best center fielders, he won three Gold Gloves for defensive excellence. In 1976, he led the league with 40 doubles and helped the Royals capture their first American League West title. Otis became a clear Kansas City fan favorite throughout his 14-year career and finished among the Royals all-time leaders in hits (1,977), home runs (193), runs scored (1,074), stolen bases (340) and games played (1,891).

Steve Busby
Pitcher 1972–1980
Inducted 1986

Coupling his amazing ability with an equally intimidating competitive fire, Busby burst onto the scene like few other pitchers. He was named the 1973 American League Rookie Pitcher of the Year in a vote by his peers. The two-time All-Star was the Royals 1974 Pitcher of the Year when he won 22 games. From 1973–75, he averaged more than 18 wins, 260 innings pitched, and 177 strikeouts. He was the first pitcher in Major League history to throw no-hitters in each of his first two seasons. Though his career was shortened by a rotator cuff injury, his achievements earned him induction in the inaugural year of the Royals Hall of Fame.

10. Ned Yost.

The Royals were not the first managerial stop for Ned Yost, but Kansas City is certainly where he perfected his own particular leadership style. Yost would say he was afforded the opportunity to take a master class in major-league managing as a member of Hall of Famer Bobby Cox's Atlanta Braves staff for 12 years from 1991 to 2002.

Yost helmed the Milwaukee Brewers from 2003 through 2008, guiding their 2007 team to that franchise's first winning

National Baseball Hall of Fame manager Whitey Herzog talks to Royals manager Ned Yost. On June 18, 2015, Yost posted his 411th win to surpass Herzog for most ever by a Royals manager with a 3–2 victory over Milwaukee at Kauffman Stadium.

record since 1992. He managed his first Royals game on May 14, 2010—a 6–1 win over the Chicago White Sox. Just a little over four years later, he surpassed Whitey Herzog for the most managerial wins in club history (411) on June 18, 2015 with a 3–2 win over Milwaukee. Both wins were at Kauffman Stadium.

In between, Yost led the Royals through a complete transformation from years of frustration to a return to championship baseball. The Royals' ascension under Yost mirrored his personality as an on-field leader, both steady and sure.

The Royals' win total increased each and every season from that first Yost victory in 2010 through the 2014 pennant-winning year and his club record 411th in 2015—the same year the ballclub captured its first division title in 30 years and then its second world championship.

Yost would join both his mentor Bobby Cox and Royals Hall of Famer Whitey Herzog in saying his players won the games. But successful teams need leaders and successful leaders instill confidence in their teams. Ned Yost believed in his players and his teams have always believed in him. The results delivered championships for Kansas City and more wins for Yost than any manager in Royals history.

11. Known as the City of Fountains, Kansas City has more fountains than any city other than Rome. The first fountains in early Kansas City served basic water needs, but as the community grew, a vast array of waterworks emerged for their artistic value alone. *But fountains in a ballpark?* For Kansas City, it was a natural fit.

The fountains concept initially belonged to Muriel Kauffman, but it didn't take much to sell her husband on the idea.

Whereas A's owner Charlie Finley had once placed a small zoo beyond the outfield wall at Municipal Stadium, the Kauffmans sought something a bit more stately for Kansas City's new baseball showplace being built in the early 1970s. The plans for Royals Stadium already had a sleek modern look, and the addition of fountains beautified the ballpark all the more. The concept was innovative, the design was majestic, and the result became iconic.

Royals Stadium's fountains were the work of Anthony C. Mifsud, who designed water displays across Europe and those at the 1964 New York World's Fair. The Water Spectacular, as it was originally known, included 120 switches that controlled eight different shows with multiple variations to each computer-controlled sequence. One single jet of water was set to reach as high as 70 feet to celebrate every Royals home run. Not believing the original design was spectacular enough, the Royals' founders invested an additional $1.5 million into the project to make the display perfect.

The end result was the largest privately funded fountain system in the world—one that held nearly half a million gallons of water and spanned more than 320 feet. Decades later, the fountains still make Kansas City's ballpark one of the most recognizable in all of sports.

Unlike its attention-grabbing crown scoreboard sibling, the Water Spectacular was not quite ready for Royals Stadium's debut on April 10, 1973, mostly due to unseasonably cold temperatures. But every inch of the 320 feet of the fountains took center stage at the 1973 All-Star Game just three months later. They have remained at center stage at Royals Stadium and now Kauffman Stadium ever since.

Did You Know?—*The game on June 25, 2002 at Kauffman Stadium was the first MLB contest between teams led by two managers from the Dominican Republic: former Royals player Luis Pujols for the Tigers and Tony Pena for the Royals.*

12. 1973.

The Royals first wore their now iconic powder blue uniforms on Opening Night at Anaheim Stadium against the Angels on April 6, 1973. The uniforms were a hit, but the Royals lost 3–2 in a tight pitchers' duel between future Royals Hall of Famer Steve Busby and future National Baseball Hall of Famer Nolan Ryan.

The original powder blue was a break from tradition and became a Kansas City trademark. Other teams wore the color in the era, but few with as much style and success as the Royals. The reasons behind the uniform color switch were varied, but the brightness and impact they made on television were most often listed as the leading factors in the decision.

The original version was a v-neck pullover jersey top with "Kansas City" in block letters arched across the chest. It was also strictly the Royals' road uniform, and was powder blue from top to bottom with elastic-waistbanded powder blue baseball pants.

The powder blue jersey had a makeover in 1983. Version 2.0 was a more traditional button-up jersey top—this time with script "Royals" across the chest and the addition of numbers on the front of the jersey as well as the back. The powder blue baseball pants also remained part of the ensemble, but were looped for a belt in another return to baseball tradition.

The Royals jettisoned the powder blues after the 1991 season and went back to gray road uniforms. But the pull and power of powder blue returned again in 2008 when the Royals reintroduced the color to a new generation of fans. This time it became a home jersey color and immediately became a fan favorite again. This time powder blue will hopefully stay as a touchstone of Royals tradition.

13. Bret Saberhagen.

Because he is remembered for so many great performances, individual awards, and championship moments, it is often overlooked that Bret Saberhagen was also the youngest player to ever appear in a Royals uniform. The future Royals Hall of Famer made his major-league debut on April 4, 1984 at the age of 19 years and 359 days old.

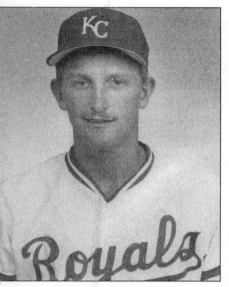

Before Saberhagen, the youngest Royals player had been Clint Hurdle, who debuted on September 18, 1977 at the age of 20 years and 50 days old. Saberhagen's debut was a 4 ⅔-inning relief outing for fellow Royals Hall of Famer Paul Splittorff in which he surrendered three hits but no runs and took a no-decision (although the Royals lost to the Yankees 4–3 at Royals Stadium). He was also the youngest-ever Royals pitcher to make a major-league start when he took the mound at Tiger

Royals Hall of Fame pitcher Bret Saberhagen made his major-league debut on April 4, 1984. At 19 years and 359 days old, he was the youngest player in Royals history.

Stadium in Detroit on April 19, 1984—just eight days after his 20th birthday.

The 1984 Detroit Tigers were the best team in baseball from start to finish. They won their first nine games. After 40 games they stood at an amazing 35-5. They finished the year 104-58 and never spent a day out of first place. They swept the American League Championship Series—against the surprise AL West Champion Royals as it turned out—and won the World Series in five games against the San Diego Padres.

But that vaunted Tigers juggernaut club's first loss of the season came at the hands of the 20-year-old pitcher in his first big-league start less than two years removed from being the ace of the Grover Cleveland High School Cavaliers in Reseda, California. Saberhagen went six innings, surrendering six hits and one earned run, walking two and striking out four.

The Tigers took the early lead, with an RBI groundout in the first by Lance Parrish. Back-to-back RBI singles from Jorge Orta and Hal McRae put the Royals in front 2–1 in the third inning. Frank White finished the Royals' scoring with a two-run home run in the eighth. Saberhagen departed with a 3–1 lead and was backed up by fellow Royals Hall of Famer Dan Quisenberry's three innings for the save. The Royals defeated the Tigers 5–2—also making Saberhagen the youngest Royals pitcher to ever record a win.

14. Lou Piniella.

Lou Piniella was the heart, soul, and fire that lit up the Royals inaugural year of 1969. Though technically a rookie, Piniella had been part of four organizations and had actually made his major-league debut five years earlier. But he finally "arrived" in Kansas City.

Piniella was first signed by the Cleveland Indians on June 9, 1962 as an amateur free agent, only to be drafted that November by the Washington Senators in the first-year draft. Not to be confused with the amateur draft that began in 1965, this first-year player draft is a little-remembered part of baseball history (1959-1964) that allowed major-league teams to select minor-league players that had just completed their initial professional season from other organizations for $15,000. He was traded to Baltimore on August 4, 1964. The Orioles were his third team and that was the charm he needed to make his major-league debut a month later, a week after his 21st birthday.

However, he only played four games before going back to the minors. Piniella was traded back to Cleveland in 1966 where he played six games for the Tribe before the Seattle Pilots selected him in the 1968 Expansion Draft. A week before the beginning of the 1969 season, the Pilots traded him to the Royals.

Five years into his professional career Piniella had played 10 major-league games. The Royals were his fifth organization in seven years, and he made a good first impression on his newest club. Manager Joe Gordon put Piniella in center field and the leadoff spot in the order for the Royals' inaugural game.

On April 8, 1969, Piniella led off the bottom of the first inning and lashed the first pitch ever thrown to a Royals hitter for a double. With the first hit in club history already to his name, he added the first run in Royals history to his ledger when Jerry Adair followed with an RBI single.

The Royals were a new beginning for Major League Baseball in Kansas City—and they were also a new beginning for Lou Piniella. From that first game with the Royals, Piniella charted an 18-year big-league career—he and Kansas City were in the major leagues to stay.

15. Kauffman Stadium changed from artificial turf to natural grass for the 1995 season.

The last game on Kauffman Stadium's artificial surface came on August 7, 1994, much earlier than anticipated due to the unresolved players strike. The work stoppage ultimately ended the baseball season, but it did allow an early jump on the ballpark's long-awaited transition to natural grass.

The project was awarded to SW Franks of Cleveland in September, and Royals Hall of Fame groundskeeper George Toma oversaw the installation. Bluegrass was the turf of choice, and the original grass came to Kansas City from Fort Morgan, Colorado, on November 11, 1994. The installations concluded that December.

The first game on Kauffman Stadium's natural grass came on April 26, 1995, a little later than anticipated after the labor stoppage extended through spring training and wasn't resolved until April 2, 1995. The ceremonial first pitch on that Opening Day fittingly went to Toma, dressed in a white tuxedo with tails.

New technologies had made the perceived advantages of artificial turf obsolete—the new grass actually drained much faster than the old carpet. The green grass was not only beautiful, but it played cooler than the concrete-based turf and was much easier on the knees of the players. For many, Kauffman Stadium's move to real grass took the ballpark from great to nearly perfect.

16. 3,154.

George Brett was the 18th player in baseball history to reach the exclusive 3,000 Hit Club, but he did not stop at that magical milestone.

In his major-league debut at Chicago's Comiskey Park on August 2, 1973, George lined out to the pitcher in his first at-bat. He came to the plate again in the top of the fourth inning and dropped a single into left field off Stan Bahnsen.

Brett's final hit came on October 3, 1993—a single off Tom Henke at Arlington Stadium in George's final major-league game. He came to the plate for the fourth and final time leading off the top of the ninth inning. Hitless in the game, he fell behind in the count 1-2 to Henke before grounding a single back up the middle. One batter later, Gary Gaetti followed with a two-run home run allowing George to score the final run of his career—without really running.

There was perfect symmetry in one respect for both hit #1 and hit #3,154 by George—they both came in games won by the Royals.

17. The 1977 Royals won 102 games.

Many say the 1977 Royals were the best team in franchise history, and there is ample evidence to support that claim. Debate can rage as to whether the 1980, 1985, or 2015 Royals rate in comparison, but 1977 was undeniably a magical season for both team success and individual accomplishments.

In one of the most overlooked performances in Royals history, outfielder Al Cowens won a Rawlings Gold Glove and finished second in American League MVP voting behind Rod Carew. Dennis Leonard led the American League with 20 wins and posted a club record with an astonishing 21 complete games (astonishing at least by today's standards). Hal McRae led the league in doubles, Fred Patek led in stolen bases, and—in a sign of things to come—Frank White won his first Gold Glove.

The 1977 Kansas City Royals won the American League Western Division with a 102-60 record. The 102 wins led the major leagues that season and stand as a Royals club record.

Although the 1977 Royals entered June 7 ½ games out of first place, they caught fire in the second half of the season. The club closed on a torrid pace, winning 38 of their last 47 games and finished with the best record in baseball, 102-60 (.630), and a second consecutive American League West title.

Those that make the case for the 1977 Royals as the best team in franchise history have many stats and numbers to back their case. And at the top of that list is the number 102—the most wins ever posted by a Royals team in any single season.

18. Royals Hall of Famers Cookie Rojas and Fred Patek.

When Royals Stadium first opened in 1973, Rojas and Patek marveled at the sight of the beautiful fountains that were the signature element of the ballpark. They were so taken with the fountains they made a promise, saying that when the Royals won a championship they would jump into the water in celebration.

Battling to dethrone Oakland for the AL West title was tough down the stretch in 1976. Kansas City's seven-game lead on September 21 had fallen to just 2 ½ games before they avoided a sweep in Oakland behind Larry Gura's 4–0 shutout on September 29. The win clinched no worse than a tie—another win or an Oakland loss would give Kansas City the crown.

On October 1, the Twins scored a ninth-inning run to beat the Royals 4–3 at Royals Stadium. But the Royals and many fans stayed to see how the A's would fare at home against the Angels. It was scoreless into the 12th inning until Rusty Torres homered to give the Angels the lead. Former Royals pitcher Dick Drago, then with the Angels, retired the A's to save a 2–0 California win. The Royals were champions!

After the Saturday game, Cookie Rojas and Fred Patek made good on their promise to leap into the fountains after the Royals had clinched their first championship. It was a dangerous stunt, as Patek acknowledged. "We jumped in there with our cleats and everything on. If he [PR director Dean Vogelaar] hadn't had the electricity turned off, we could've been swimming out there like a couple of dead goldfish."

The Royals lost to the Twins again that afternoon, but no one cared. Whitey Herzog explained it best: "Pretty tough to get going this morning. We partied until about 4:30 a.m."

19. Bo Jackson and Eric Hosmer.

George Brett put it rather succinctly when he said of Bo Jackson, "This is not a normal guy." Nothing about Bo was "normal"—not the talent, not the stardom, and not the attention. He was already a pop culture icon when he took center stage at the 1989 Major League Baseball All-Star Game in Anaheim.

Fans left little doubt who they wanted to see starring for the American League at the Midsummer Classic. Bo was the leading AL vote-getter (1,748,696), becoming the first Royals player not named George Brett voted into the starting lineup since Darrell Porter and Frank White a decade earlier. Oakland A's manager Tony La Russa considered his options and made the unorthodox choice of batting Bo in the leadoff spot. And why not? Bo was the guy everyone wanted to see.

The National League had Oakland pitcher Dave Stewart on the ropes with two quick runs in the top of the first inning. With two outs and runners at second and third, they were threatening for more when the Dodgers' Pedro Guerrero hit a sinking fly ball into left-center field. Only a meteor out of left field stopped the American League from trailing 4–0—that meteor was Bo Jackson streaking in to make the catch. There is a baseball cliché that a player who makes a good defensive play to end an inning seems to often lead off the next—and that's exactly what was about to happen.

The great Vin Scully was at the microphone for NBC and was joined that next half-inning by former president Ronald Reagan. The two briefly talked about the president's early career as a sports broadcaster and the unique two-sport star who was coming to bat. They talked over the first pitch from National League starter Rick Reuschel—a sinker low and away. The next pitch was another sinker. *BOOM!*

Bo launched a monumental drive to center field estimated to have traveled 448 feet, but it seemed like much more.

The president was so struck by the blast he muttered only an awe-inspired "Hey!", and Scully captured the moment exclaiming, *"And look at that one, Bo Jackson says hello!"*

Hello indeed. Even Nike got the timing right. In one of the most perfect unscripted moments in American pop culture history, the famous Nike "Bo Knows" commercial aired for the first time immediately after that half-inning. Jackson added another hit, RBI, and also mixed in a stolen base in the 5–3 American League win. Bo was named 1989 All-Star Game MVP.

For all Eric Hosmer had already accomplished in his career—Royals Player of the Year, Rawlings Gold Glove Awards, a World Series win—he was still looking for the chance to add All-Star to his honor roll and finally got that chance in 2016. He made the most of it.

Hosmer was the first Royals first baseman ever elected as an American League All-Star starter. But that was only the beginning. In his first All-Star at-bat, Hosmer blasted a second-inning home run off former teammate Johnny Cueto to tie the game 1–1. And like Bo nearly three decades earlier, Eric wasn't done.

In the third inning, his RBI single scored Edwin Encarnacion to put the American League ahead 4–1. Royals manager Ned Yost kept his first baseman in the game for six innings—with a nudge from backup Miguel Cabrera, who wanted Hosmer to get a third at-bat to try for more. Hosmer wound up going 2-for-3 with a homer and two RBIs, leading the American League to a 4–2 win at Petco Park in San Diego.

His starring role in his Midsummer Classic debut ended with Hosmer earning 2016 All-Star Game Most Valuable Player honors. It was one more accomplishment for the constellation of star-making moments in Eric Hosmer's Kansas City career.

Another would be to forever have his name linked to the legend of Bo Jackson. Bo and Hoz—Royals fans will never forget their dynamic duo of All-Star Game Most Valuable Players.

20. Omaha, and only Omaha, has been the Royals Triple-A affiliate from the very beginning.

Like Kansas City, Omaha has its own unique baseball history that goes back into the 19th century. In fact, Kansas City and Omaha were rivals as far back as 1888 in the Western Association. Go back in time and you could have watched the Kansas City Blues with Western Association batting champion Jon "Spud" Johnson face off against 30-game-winner Tom Lovett of the Omaha Omahogs.

But in the 20th century, and now into the 21st, there have been precious few constants throughout all of Kansas City Royals history—but one of them is the franchise's connection to Omaha. Over these many years the Royals minor-league system has included clubs in nearly 40 locations north, south, east, and west—from Winnipeg, Manitoba, to the Dominican Republic; from San Jose, California, to Wilmington, Delaware. But the Royals Triple-A affiliate has always been in Omaha, just a little under 200 miles north of home.

With rare exceptions, nearly all the major-league players developed by the Kansas City Royals have spent some time playing in Omaha. Look back at that first 1969 Omaha roster and you'll find future Royals Hall of Famer Paul Splittorff. From Frank White, Willie Wilson, Dan Quisenberry, and George Brett to Mike Sweeney, Zack Greinke, Eric Hosmer, and Salvador Perez—they all played in Omaha. The Kansas City–Omaha connection is the longest-standing Triple-A affiliation in all of Major League Baseball.

21. Dane Iorg is the answer, but there is so much more to the story.

OK, hang with me here. This is one of the pivotal games and moments in all of Royals history, and there has always been too much of the story that goes untold. There has been quite a bit of revisionism over the years; I'll try to give a full accounting of the sequence of events every Royals fan should know by heart.

It was Saturday, October 26, 1985—Game 6 of the 1985 World Series at Royals Stadium in Kansas City. The "Miracle on I-70" as it is now remembered (at least on the western side of the Show-Me State) included great pitching, some interesting strategy, several key clutch hits, and yes, an influential missed call (or two).

We here in Kansas City are just going to have to get over it and remember only the course of the game was influenced and not the outcome of the entire series. Umpires sometimes miss calls, it's as simple as that; they're human and just because the World Series is coming down to the wire doesn't make them any more omnipotent.

Yes, with the naked eye, I thought Frank White was out trying to steal second base in the fourth inning just like umpire Bill Williams. But when you look at the video, Ozzie Smith missed tagging Frank's right leg and by the time he collided with his hip, Frank's foot had reached the bag. He was safe! Of course had Frank been called safe then Pat Sheridan's single that followed would have probably scored him and the circumstances of the game might have been different. But the Royals needed to keep their composure and stay in the game, because the series didn't end with that play. But that is probably not a close call you've ever heard discussed. Not that it mattered, or did it? I guess we'll never know.

Nor did the game, much less the series, end in the ninth inning on another missed call, despite decades of revisionist history. But before we get to that let's remember this was a great pitchers' duel with Danny Cox and Charlie Leibrandt matching shutout inning for shutout inning until the top of the eighth.

It was the Cardinals' Brian Harper who looped a clutch two-out pinch-hit RBI single into center to drive in the game's first run. A frustrated and dejected Charlie Leibrandt then walked Ozzie Smith to load the bases for National League batting champion Willie McGee. Dick Howser countered with Dan Quisenberry, who got McGee to ground into a force-out to end the threat. The Cardinals had a chance to punch a hole in the game, and the Royals bullpen ace turned them away as he did again in the ninth.

In the bottom of the ninth, Whitey Herzog summoned his closer Todd Worrell to protect a 1–0 lead. Dick Howser went to his bench of professional hitters for some clutch at-bats in the tightest of circumstances. The first up was Jorge Orta, who bounced a ball to first base and reached on a missed call. That he was out is certain. That the game would continue whether he was called safe or out is also certain. The game would not have ended on that play and it did not end on that play. Here is what followed:

- Jack Clark misplayed a foul pop, which should have retired Steve Balboni
- Steve Balboni singled to left
- Jim Sundberg laid down a sacrifice bunt attempt with two strikes; Orta was forced at third base

The Orta out at third would be the only out recorded in the inning. That is correct, Jorge Orta—called safe on a missed call at first—ended up being the only out the Cardinals put on the scoreboard in the tense bottom of the ninth inning. Then came one of the most important parts of the entire sequence. With Hal McRae pinch-hitting, Darrell Porter was charged with a passed ball, allowing both runners to move into scoring position. Here is what happened next:

Dane Iorg waves to the crowd after his pinch-hit two-RBI single in the bottom of the ninth inning gave the Royals a 2–1 walkoff win in 1985 World Series Game 6 at Royals Stadium (October 26, 1985).

- Hal McRae was walked intentionally
- Dane Iorg lofted the clutchest of clutch hits into right field
- Pinch-runner Onix Concepcion scored the tying run
- Jim Sundberg made a perfect slide to score the winning run

With a combination of strong relief pitching, luck, opportunity, strategic managerial chess, and some veteran at-bats, the Royals had tied the series at three games apiece.

Luckily for both teams no single missed call ever ended a game in the series—there was always a chance to persevere and win. All of which led to baseball's ultimate big-game opportunity for the Cardinals and Royals, Game 7 of the World Series. There was another game to play, and the Royals won that one too.

22. Christian Colon.

In retrospect, it often feels like the Royals' run to their 2015 world championship was simply destined to happen. As easy as it is to feel that way in the afterglow, none of it was scripted. The result was always in doubt and required top performances from the entire 25-man roster. Case in point—Christian Colon.

The Royals lost the first game of the 2015 American League Division Series at Kauffman Stadium and trailed in Game 2 before rallying to get the series even. In Houston, they were four runs down and six outs away from being eliminated before mounting another furious rally to get the series even in Game 4. They came home and won the deciding Game 5 to advance to the American League Championship Series. Christian Colon did not play in any of the five games of the 2015 ALDS.

The Royals defeated the Toronto Blue Jays in Game 1 and Game 2 of the 2015 American League Championship Series at Kauffman Stadium. They then went to Toronto and slammed their way to a Game 4 win, although they lost Game 3 and Game 5. They returned to Kauffman Stadium and won a thrilling Game 6 to capture their second consecutive American League pennant. Christian Colon did not play in any of the six games of the 2015 ALCS.

The Royals defeated the New York Mets in Game 1 and Game 2 of the 2015 World Series at Kauffman Stadium. They then went to New York and lost Game 3, before rebounding to win Game 4 with a three-run rally in the top of the eighth inning at Citi Field. The Royals and Mets were four games into the 2015 World Series, and Christian Colon had not yet played in any of the four.

In Game 5, the Royals were scoreless into the top of the ninth inning before another thrilling rally plated two runs to get the contest tied. The game went into extra innings. Through 10 innings, still no Christian Colon. Through 11 innings, still no Christian Colon.

In the 12th inning, with the go-ahead run at second in a potential World Series–clinching opportunity, Royals manager Ned Yost went to his bench to pinch-hit for pitcher Luke Hochevar. The pinch-hitter was none other than Christian Colon, the same Christian Colon who had not had an official game at-bat since the Royals' last regular-season contest nearly a month earlier on October 4 (in which he singled).

Colon fell behind in the count to Addison Reed 1-2. He fouled off a fourth pitch, then delivered an RBI single scoring pinch-runner Jarrod Dyson to give the Royals the lead. It was the start of a five-run rally that clinched the second world championship in Kansas City Royals history.

Christian Colon proved nothing about the Royals' 2015 run could possibly have been scripted—it would have been unbelievable. The championship required every man on the 25-man roster.

23. July 2, 1993.

Since 1993, the home of the Royals has simply been "The K" to many fans as a tribute to club founder Ewing Kauffman, who was affectionately known as Mr. K. But the man himself was never in any hurry to have the honor—in fact, he put the brakes on the idea several times.

In what would be his last appearance at Royals Stadium, Ewing Kauffman was inducted into the Royals Hall of Fame on May 23, 1993. The ballpark was officially renamed Kauffman Stadium on July 2, 1993, although Mr. Kauffman was too ill to attend the ceremonies.

Kauffman brushed off the first effort in 1981, and again after a second move by the Jackson County Legislature in 1988. He said many times that having his name on things made of "bricks and mortar" was something he did not want or need. Although, to be clear, he appreciated that his contributions would be deemed worthy of such an honor by the people in his hometown. Mr. Kauffman firmly believed his legacy—whatever it might be—would be forged in the things he did, and the people he inspired. And so, the ballpark remained Royals Stadium.

After Mr. Kauffman announced he had a recurrence of bone cancer in June of 1993, the issue was raised a third time. As he entered the final days of his life, it was his wife who prevailed upon him to finally accept the honor. Kauffman said at the time, "Muriel's the one who put the pressure on and persuaded me to change my mind, which she's highly capable of doing."

On July 2, 1993 the ballpark was officially named Ewing M. Kauffman Stadium, though the man himself was then too ill to attend. Interestingly, for all the years Mr. K watched games perched in his box at Royals Stadium, he would never set foot into it as Kauffman Stadium. He passed away on August 1, 1993.

24. Eight, and it should have been nine (if not more).

Frank White won his first Rawlings Gold Glove after the 1977 season—his second as the Royals' primary starter at second base. It was Royals manager Whitey Herzog who made the tough decision to transition fan-favorite Cookie Rojas to a utility role to free up second base for the young Kansas City native named Frank White. Herzog summed up his thoughts on Frank White's abilities this way: "There are four things you want a second baseman to do: go left, go right, come in, and go out. Frank could do those four things better than any second baseman I have ever seen."

Frank played with such grace and style that he earned the nickname "Smooth"—which was just about the perfect moniker for him. During that 1977 season, Frank played 62 consecutive games without an error and took home his first Gold Glove, which started a string of six consecutive seasons (1977–1982) in which he won the honors.

He followed up those first six Gold Gloves with two more in 1986 and 1987, becoming the first American League second baseman to earn the honor eight times. Whitey Herzog was proven correct.

In fact, many feel White should have earned the award again in 1988 when he led all American League second basemen, posting the highest fielding percentage of his career at .994, making just four errors in 723 chances. He finished second in a close vote behind the Mariners' Harold Reynolds, who would go on to capture three Gold Gloves in his career.

25. Two—1973 and 2012.

Royals Stadium hosted its first All-Star Game in 1973 during the inaugural year of the ballpark—although it was the second held in Kansas City. The Athletics hosted the first All-Star Game in Kansas City in 1960 at Municipal Stadium.

The 1973 All-Star Game served as the first real national showcase for brand-new Royals Stadium. The game also marked the 40th anniversary of the first All-Star Game, played in 1933 at Comiskey Park in Chicago. Several National Baseball Hall of Famers who played in that very first Midsummer Classic made appearances at the 1973 contest, including Joe Cronin, Charlie Gehringer, Carl Hubbell, and Lefty Gomez.

The All-Star Game was played for the second time in Kansas City on July 24, 1973 at brand-new Royals Stadium. Bobby Bonds of the San Francisco Giants was named the MVP in the National League's 7–1 victory.

Played on July 24, 1973, the game was dominated by three long home runs off the bats of Johnny Bench of the Cincinnati Reds, Bobby Bonds of the San Francisco Giants, and Willie Davis of the Los Angeles Dodgers—all for the National League in their 7–1 victory. Although not a starter in the game, Bonds also doubled and would be named the game's Most Valuable Player.

The renovations of Kauffman Stadium completed in 2009 assured Kansas City another All-Star Game. Major League Baseball announced in 2010 that Kansas City would host the 2012 All-Star Game. At the time, the honor gave the "The K" the distinction of being one of only four ballparks still in use to host multiple All-Star Games—joining Angel Stadium, Wrigley Field, and Fenway Park.

After a 39-year hiatus, Kansas City hosted its third All-Star Game on July 10, 2012 at Kauffman Stadium. Melky Cabrera of the San Francisco Giants was named the MVP in the National League's 8–0 victory.

Played on July 10, 2012, the game was decided early with a five-run top of the first inning by the National League highlighted by a bases-loaded triple by Pablo Sandoval of the San Francisco Giants. Former Royals player Melky Cabrera, then with the Giants, hit the only home run and was named the game's MVP.

The 8–0 National League victory made the Senior Circuit a perfect 3-0 in Kansas City–hosted All-Star Games. The win gave the National League home-field advantage in the World Series. And powered as it was by Giants players, it was fitting that the edge was used by San Francisco to sweep Detroit in the 2012 World Series.

VETERAN LEVEL

1. Name the three teams besides the Royals who were part of the 1969 MLB expansion. *Answer on page 51.*

2. When George Brett won his first American League batting title in 1976, which of his teammates placed right behind him in second? *Answer on page 52.*

3. What Royals pitcher holds the record for most career strikeouts? *Answer on page 53.*

4. What team did the Royals play against in the 1976, 1977, 1978, and 1980 ALCS? *Answer on page 55.*

5. Who scored the winning run in the American League Wild Card Game in 2014? *Answer on page 58.*

6. How many times have the Royals had the overall number one pick in the June draft? *Answer on page 60.*

7. Who holds the record for most career saves in Royals history? *Answer on page 60.*

8. What year did Mike Sweeney set a team record with 144 RBIs? *Answer on page 62.*

9. Who was the first (and, through 2016, the only) member of the Royals to lead the American League in RBIs? *Answer on page 63.*

10. What is the highest jersey number worn by a Royals player? *Answer on page 64.*

11. Who was the first Japanese-born player to play for the Royals? *Answer on page 64.*

12. Who was the first player in Royals history to wear the jersey number 0? *Answer on page 66.*

13. According to the Royals record book, what was the longest home run ever hit at Royals/Kauffman Stadium? *Answer on page 67.*

14. One of the most memorable plays in the highlight reel career of Bo Jackson was a stunning throw to home to nail a runner at the plate. Who did Bo Jackson throw out at the plate with his outfield wall to home plate cannon shot known as "The Throw"? *Answer on page 69.*

15. What player holds the Royals record for most RBIs in a single game? *Answer on page 71.*

16. What player holds the Royals record for most stolen bases in a single game? *Answer on page 72.*

17. What pitcher surrendered the first career home run by George Brett? *Answer on page 73.*

18. How many career home runs did George Brett have? *Answer on page 75.*

19. How many pitchers have won 100 games in a Kansas City Royals uniform? *Answer on page 76.*

20. Who was the first player to hit a home run for the Kansas City Royals? *Answer on page 78.*

21. What Royals player holds the major-league record for stolen bases in a single season by a catcher? *Answer on page 80.*

22. Who hit both the last home run for the Royals at Municipal Stadium and the first ever at Royals Stadium? *Answer on page 82.*

23. Who is the oldest player to ever hit a home run for the Royals? *Answer on page 84.*

24. Who is the youngest player to ever hit a home run for the Royals? *Answer on page 86.*

25. In how many seasons have the Royals posted the most wins in the American League? *Answer on page 89.*

VETERAN LEVEL — ANSWERS

1. Seattle Pilots, San Diego Padres, and Montreal Expos.

The 1969 expansion added more teams than any other expansion in Major League Baseball history. Both the National League and American League added two new franchises, and the ramifications of the added teams changed the face of the game forever.

The American League went first by announcing their expansion plan to add two teams on October 18, 1967. The timetable was spurred along by the Kansas City delegation at the American League owners meeting that had originally called for expansion "some time not later than 1971." Kansas City's pressure to up the schedule worked and 1969 would be the year. The expansion franchises were awarded to Kansas City and first-time big-league market Seattle.

The National League followed suit on May 27, 1968 with the announcement of their plans to field expansion teams in San Diego and Montreal—both markets new to Major League Baseball. The expansion into Canada was the first-ever foray by Major League Baseball outside of the United States.

With the additions, both leagues would include 12 teams each and the sheer number of clubs also brought about another altogether new wrinkle to Major League Baseball—divisional play. Both leagues would divide themselves into divisions for the first time and, by doing so, would usher in the era of play-offs with the addition of the League Championship Series.

For the first time ever, the World Series would not be the only round of postseason play.

The Royals would be the most successful of the four entries, posting a winning campaign in just their third year (1971), their first division championship in year eight (1976), their first league pennant in year 12 (1980), and their first world championship in year 17 (1985). Together, the Royals' three sibling expansion franchises didn't record their first winning season until a decade later, their first divisional title 13 years later, their first league pennant 14 years later—and none of the other three have won a world championship.

Also of note, only the San Diego Padres still remain in their original hometown. The Seattle Pilots moved one year later to become the Milwaukee Brewers—they later changed leagues, moving from the American League to the National League in 1998. The Montreal Expos became the Washington Nationals in 2005.

2. Hal McRae.

George Brett's first batting title was by far the fiercest battle of his three. The chase went down to the final game of the 1976 season—indeed it went well into that final game of the season. The Royals had already clinched their first American League Western Division title and were finishing out the season in what could have been viewed as a meaningless game against Minnesota at Royals Stadium. But it was perhaps one of the most meaningful meaningless games ever played, because the top four contenders for the American League batting title were on the field, all separated by just a few percentage points.

As the game began, Brett (.331) and Hal McRae (.331) of the Royals along with Rod Carew (.327) and Lyman Bostock

(.323) of the Twins were all within .008 points of each other. Bostock would miss the game with a thumb injury, so his number was set. The other three were ready for a battle to the finish.

Carew had his final at-bat in the top of the ninth inning and singled. He finished the game 2-for-4 and moved his batting average to .331. Both Royals would come to bat in the bottom of the ninth, with Brett already 2-for-3 in the game with his average at .332298; McRae was 2-for-3 and his average was .332699—the difference was down to the fourth decimal point.

Brett was up second and lofted a fly ball that eluded left fielder Steve Brye. While Brye and center fielder Larry Hisle chased the baseball, Brett circled the bases for an inside-the-park home run. The hit moved Brett's batting average to .333333, just in front of McRae. The Royals designated hitter grounded out to shortstop, dropping his average to .332068. McRae was incensed, not because his teammate got a hit, but because he believed Brye had misplayed the ball on purpose to deny McRae the batting title—with the complicity of Twins manager Gene Mauch. The accusation by McRae (an African American) had racial overtones (Brett, Brye, and Mauch were white). The insinuation was vehemently denied by Mauch, who claimed he was mad at Brye for playing Brett so deep.

The eyelash finish was bittersweet for Brett because of the battle with his friend and teammate. George won his first batting title with a difference of .001265. The game was meaningful even if the score was meaningless. The Twins won 5–3, but the Royals had their first-ever American League batting champion in George Brett.

3. Kevin Appier.

Selected in the first round of the 1987 June draft, Robert Kevin Appier continued the Royals' strong tradition of developing pitchers started by Paul Splittorff and continued by Dennis Leonard, Bret Saberhagen, and others. He made his Royals debut in 1989, starting a decade-plus run as one of the best pitchers of his era.

Appier became the foundation of the Royals starting rotation during his 1990 rookie season when he posted a 12-8 record with three shutouts and finished third in American League Rookie of the Year voting. It truly was just the start for one of the best pitchers in Royals history.

In 1993, Appier set a Royals record for most consecutive scoreless innings with 33 and had two six-game winning streaks en route to an 18-8 record. He also led the league with a 2.56 ERA and finished third in American League Cy Young balloting.

The 1995 All-Star was traded to Oakland on July 31, 1999 and eventually played for the Mets and Angels before returning to Kansas City in 2003 and 2004. Appier concluded his career as the Royals' all-time strikeout leader with 1,458. He was a nearly unanimous choice for the Royals Hall of Fame in 2011.

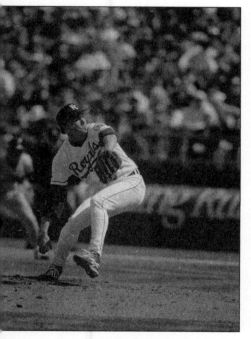

Royals Hall of Fame pitcher Kevin Appier holds the club career strikeouts record with 1,458. Appier had two stints with the Royals, the first at the start of his career from 1989 to 1999 and then again at the close from 2003 to 2004.

His Royals Hall of Fame plaque reads:

Kevin Appier
Pitcher 1989–1999; 2003–2004
Inducted 2011

His one-of-a-kind delivery and devastating mix of pitches made Appier one of the dominant pitchers of his era. The three-time Royals Pitcher of the Year retired as the club's all-time strikeout leader with 1,458. He made more Opening Day starts (7) than any Kansas City pitcher before him. Appier posted the lowest ERA (2.56) in the league in 1993 and was named to the 1995 American League All-Star team. He also threw a pair of one-hit games and finished his career among the Royals Top 10 in almost every pitching category including wins (115), ERA (3.49), shutouts (10), games started (275), and innings pitched (1,843.2).

4. New York Yankees.

There was a time when the New York Yankees were not baseball Enemy Number One in Kansas City. But starting with the Athletics era and into Royals history, that all changed. When the Royals first came of age and started winning championships to reach postseason play, the Yankees became an obstacle—much to our frustration, a consistent and repeating obstacle, which made defeating them almost an obsession.

For nearly 20 years, from 1936 to 1954, Kansas City was home to one of the New York Yankees' top farm affiliates. The Kansas City Blues played in the American Association, and the rosters from those teams included some of the greatest Yankees of all time, including Mickey Mantle (1951), Whitey Ford (1950), and Yogi Berra (1944–1945), among others. Even the immortal Casey Stengel, a Kansas City native himself, managed the Blues in 1945 before heading to the Bronx, where he led the Yankees to 10 American League pennants and seven World Series titles between 1949 and 1960.

All that was literally and figuratively ancient history when the Royals won their first American League Western Division title in 1976. Those Royals would square off against none other than the New York Yankees in the American League Championship Series. It was of course the Royals' first-ever postseason appearance, but it also ended a 12-season postseason drought for the vaunted Yankees.

The 1976 ALCS was a thriller going all the way to a winner-take-all fifth and deciding game at Yankee Stadium.

Yankees manager Billy Martin and Royals manager Whitey Herzog exchange their lineup cards with the umpires before 1976 American League Championship Series Game 2 in Kansas City. The Royals won the game 7–3 for the first postseason victory in club history.

The Royals scored three runs in the top of the eighth on a three-run home run by George Brett to tie the game. But Chris Chambliss hit the first pitch in the bottom of the ninth to win the pennant for New York.

The Royals earned their way back in 1977 and so did the Yankees. In round two between Kansas City and New York, the series again went to a fifth and deciding game. This time the Royals led 3–2 entering the ninth inning at Royals Stadium. Unfortunately, the Yankees rallied for two runs to take the lead and the Royals once again just missed a chance at the World Series.

Not again. Yes, the very next year the same two teams faced off in the 1978 ALCS. Despite George Brett's Game 3 performance with three home runs off the Yankees' Catfish Hunter, the Royals only found heartache again—falling to New York in four games.

Then came 1980. The Royals were back in the playoffs for the fourth time in five years, and awaiting them for a fourth in five years were those same New York Yankees. Curses, not the dang Yankees again!

But after three heart-wrenching ALCS losses, perhaps there was no better matchup for the Royals and Royals fans. This time the series lasted just three games—and finally ended with tears of joy in Kansas City. The Royals won the first two at home, and then traveled to Yankee Stadium for Game 3. Frank White's fifth-inning solo home run got the Royals started, but they trailed 2–1 in the seventh. George Brett's three-run home run on a Goose Gossage fastball into the upper deck cleared the way for the Royals. Dan Quisenberry closed the door in the bottom of the ninth inning with a strikeout of Willie Randolph and the Royals completed the sweep. The Kansas City Royals were American League champions.

The Royals' first 17 postseason games all came against the Yankees over the course of five years. Through the 2016 season, the two franchises have not matched up in postseason play since. If you were around to experience it, beating the Yankees for the 1980 American League pennant was one of the most exhilarating and cathartic moments in Royals history.

5. Christian Colon.

For those who didn't experience the exhilarating and cathartic moment of beating the Yankees to capture the 1980 American League pennant, a similar feeling came to Royals fans during the aptly named Wild Card playoff game of 2014. The Royals were in the postseason for the first time in 29 years, and for a time it felt like the fun would last just a few hours— then it became a series of moments that will live forever.

It was the first postseason game at Kauffman Stadium since Royals Stadium had hosted Game 7 of the 1985 World Series on October 27, 1985. Although completely different games, those two contests would both become vivid memories for all who saw them.

The Wild Card Game was played on Tuesday, September 30, and when the game began, no team had ever had seven different players steal a base in the same postseason game. When the game ended, Nori Aoki, Alcides Escobar, Lorenzo Cain, Terrance Gore, Alex Gordon, Jarrod Dyson, and Christian Colon all had stolen bases—and five of them scored.

When the game began, no team in Major League Baseball history had come back down four runs in the eighth inning or later of a winner-take-all playoff game. When the game ended, the Royals had done just that. *And they came from behind again in the 12th inning.*

Christian Colon, who had driven in the tying run, scored the winning run on Salvador Perez's 12th-inning walkoff single in the American League Wild Card Game against Oakland on September 30, 2014. The 9–8 victory was the first Royals postseason game since winning Game 7 of the 1985 World Series.

After rallying twice to catch Oakland, from down 2–0 after the top of the first and later down 7–3 after the sixth—the Royals fell behind again 8–7 in the 12th. It only set up another first when the Royals became the first team to have both game-tying and game-ending extra-innings hits in a winner-take-all playoff game.

Sal Perez scored Christian Colon with a two-out RBI single in the 12th for the 9–8 walkoff win over Oakland in front of a delirious Kauffman Stadium crowd. When the game began it was September. When the game ended it was October. It was exhilarating. It was thrilling. It was Kansas City back in the postseason with a win in the wildest, most amazing way—and Christian Colon scored the winning run.

6. Once.

The Royals have only had the overall number one pick in the June draft one time. Because the draft order is based on the records of major-league teams in the preceding year, the fact the Royals have only held the top position in the draft once is a good thing in the aggregate. The one occasion followed the 2005 season, in which the Royals finished with a forgettable 56-106 record.

As a result, the Royals had the first selection in the draft for the first time in franchise history. On June 6, 2006 the Royals selected right-handed pitcher Luke Anthony Hochevar, then playing with the American Association Independent League Fort Worth Cats.

Hochevar was actually a re-draft, as he had been the first-round selection of the Los Angeles Dodgers with the 40th overall pick in the 2005 June draft. He didn't sign and re-entered the draft. In fact, it was the second time Hochevar had not signed with the Dodgers, as they had also selected him in the 39th round of the 2002 June draft, but he instead decided to attend the University of Tennessee in Knoxville.

Did You Know?—*The first player ever drafted by the Royals was shortstop Kenneth O'Donnell from Neptune High School (Neptune, New Jersey) in the fourth round of the 1968 June draft—see if you can win a bet with that one. O'Donnell finished his career in 1972 with the Royals Double-A affiliate Jacksonville Suns of the Southern League.*

7. Jeff Montgomery.

Jeff Montgomery debuted with his boyhood favorite team the Reds in 1987 after being Cincinnati's ninth-round selection in the 1983 June draft out of Marshall University in

Huntington, West Virginia. The native of Wellston, Ohio—located in southern Ohio, about 125 miles east of Cincinnati—pitched in 14 games for the Reds in 1987 before his trade to Kansas City on February 15, 1988.

The move was unquestionably bittersweet, as he was leaving the dream of playing for his favorite team in his home state. But it was also a new opportunity in Kansas City, and decades later he remains a Kansas Citian. The trade worked out in nearly every way for both Montgomery and the Royals—for the Reds, not so much.

It took a while, but not all that long, for him to get settled in Kansas City. Montgomery made his Royals debut on June 4, 1988 and recorded his first career save four days later on June 8—although it was his first and only save of the 1988 season. He really took over the closer role during the 1989 season and was one of the best in all of baseball for the remainder of his career.

Monty was an unconventional closer in some ways. Where many relievers rely on power or a single outstanding pitch, Montgomery maximized his true four-pitch arsenal. The results were undeniable. By the time his career concluded in 1999, Montgomery had set a Royals franchise record with 304 saves. He was the 10th pitcher in baseball history to reach the 300 career save mark, and the first to collect them all with one team.

His Royals Hall of Fame plaque reads:

Jeff Montgomery
Pitcher 1989–1999
Inducted 2003

Breaking the traditional closer mold, Montgomery became one of the most reliable relief aces in baseball. The three-time All-Star and 1998 Royals Pitcher of the Year led the club in

saves for a decade with an unconventional four-pitch reper-
toire. In 1993, he was American League Fireman of the Year
with a league-leading 45 saves, which also tied the Royals club
record. Montgomery was Major League Baseball's 10th pitcher
to reach the 300-plus saves mark, and the first to collect all of
them with one club. He finished his career atop the Royals all-
time list in appearances (686) and saves (304).

8. 2000.

Mike Sweeney turned 18 on July 22, 1991, a big day mark-
ing his leap into adulthood. But unlike most 18-year-olds, he
was also starting a professional baseball career that would land
him in the Royals Hall of Fame.

The Royals selected Michael John Sweeney in the 10th
round of the 1991 June draft. As a high school senior he hit
.458, leading his Ontario Jaguars to a perfect 26-0 record and
a California State Championship. Sweeney had committed to
play ball at Cal-State Fullerton, but decided to cast his lot professionally with the Royals.

He started in the Gulf Coast League in 1991—hitting .216
in 38 games. Sweeney hit .221 with Single-A Eugene in 1992.
In 1993, he was a Northwest League All-Star at Eugene and his
rise began. With Rockford, he hit .301 and was named a 1994
Midwest League All-Star. The next year he won the Carolina
League batting title (.310) with Single-A Wilmington—from
there he made his MLB debut on September 4, 1995.

Sweeney split two seasons bouncing between the minors
and Kansas City—arriving for good on July 10, 1997. He was
catcher Mike Macfarlane's backup, and then shared duties with
Sal Fasano in 1998. The crucible of Sweeney's career was 1999
when he was the Royals' third catcher. An injury to DH Jeremy

Giambi and first baseman Jeff King's in-season retirement gave Sweeney a new opportunity. He made the most of it.

He led the team with a .322 batting average that year and would eventually be named an American League All-Star five times. It was the year following his breakout campaign of 1999 that Sweeney set the Royals single-season record with 144 RBIs.

9. Hal McRae.

Mike Sweeney holds the Royals single-season record for RBI (144), but he didn't lead the American League that season, as Edgar Martinez of the Seattle Mariners finished with one more. The first Royals player to lead the American League in RBIs was the fellow Royals Hall of Famer who held the Royals single-season record before Sweeney. Hal McRae topped the American League with 133 RBIs in 1982, far outdistancing the second best of 121 by Cecil Cooper of the Milwaukee Brewers.

McRae debuted with the Royals on April 6, 1973 after being acquired in a trade from the Cincinnati Reds on November 30, 1972. He was an outfielder by trade and started there in his Royals career. However, the 1973 season was the first year the American League used the designated-hitter rule. As it turned out, it was perfect timing for McRae. It wasn't until 1976 that McRae became the Royals' full-time DH, but he took to the position like few others and became one of the first stars to flourish in that new role.

Although McRae was a rock-steady run producer for the Royals during his 15 seasons in Kansas City, his 1982 campaign was his one and only with 100 or more RBIs. McRae did record 1,012 RBIs during his Royals career, one of only two players to reach the 1,000 mark in franchise history.

10. 91.

Hideo Nomo was a star before he ever threw a major-league pitch. He was a member of Japan's silver-medal–winning baseball team at the 1988 Summer Olympic Games in Seoul, South Korea. The following year he was drafted by the Osaka Kintetsu Buffaloes of Japan's highest professional league—Nippon Professional Baseball.

From 1990 to 1994, Nomo was one of Japan's most dominant pitchers, collecting 78 wins in a little over four full seasons. In 1995, he signed with the Los Angeles Dodgers and became only the second Japanese-born player to ever appear in Major League Baseball. The first was another pitcher, Masanori Murakami with the 1964 San Francisco Giants.

Nomo's unique pitching style—turning his back to home plate with his pivot leg raised and an exaggerated pause at the top of his windup—gave him his nickname, "The Tornado." Nomo was a sensation, winning 1995 National League Rookie of the Year honors.

He later pitched for six other big-league clubs, finishing his career with three appearances as a member of the 2008 Kansas City Royals. It was a storied career, but those three appearances with the Royals weren't very memorable, as he allowed nine runs on 10 hits over the course of 4 ⅓ innings.

Still, the 39-year-old Nomo did make his way into the Royals record book with his jersey number alone. He went to the mound wearing number 91, which was the highest number ever worn by a Royals player.

11. Mac Suzuki.

Mac Suzuki was just the third Japanese-born player to play Major League Baseball when he debuted with the Seattle

Mariners on July 7, 1996. But it was Suzuki's path to the big leagues that really made his story unique.

Born and raised in Kobe, Japan, Suzuki's parents sent him to the United States after he was kicked out of high school. He admitted that the dismissal was probably appropriate, saying: "I was a bad kid." The 16-year-old came to California in 1992 and landed a job as a clubhouse kid and batboy for the Single-A California League Salinas Peppers managed by his fellow countryman Hidehiko Koga. Suzuki pitched for the Peppers in the final game of the season and the next year for the San Bernardino Spirit, warranting enough attention to be signed by the Seattle Mariners organization.

Three years later Suzuki was in the big leagues with the Mariners. He later played for the Rockies, Brewers, and had two stints in Kansas City with the Royals between 1999 and 2002. He was the first, and remains the only, Japanese-born player to reach the major leagues in America without having started his career in Japanese professional baseball.

The Royals selected Suzuki off waivers from the New York Mets on June 22, 1999. He made his Royals debut in relief of starter Chris Fussell, who had allowed six runs over the first two innings of a game against Cleveland at Kauffman Stadium. Suzuki pitched three innings, allowing one run on three hits. The Royals rallied from down 7–0 with a run in the seventh and exploded for 10 runs in the eighth inning to win the game 11–7.

On June 24, 2001, the Royals traded Suzuki along with catcher Sal Fasano to the Colorado Rockies to reacquire former Royals catcher Brent Mayne. Suzuki would also be reacquired by the Royals when he was signed as a free agent on December 3, 2001, and he made seven more appearances in 2002.

In an interesting twist, Suzuki did finally pitch briefly in the Nippon Baseball League back in his home country. He pitched for the Orix Blue Wave in 2003 and 2004—then continued to pitch in the Mexican League, making his last appearance in 2010. He seemed to live by the motto, "Have arm, will travel."

Did You Know?—*When Paulo Orlando debuted for the Royals on April 9, 2015, he became only the third Brazilian-born player to ever appear in Major League Baseball. The first was Yan Gomes, who is the son-in-law of former Royals pitcher Atlee Hammaker.*

12. George "Boomer" Scott.

The Royals acquired George Scott on June 13, 1979 in one of the more unusual trades in club history. Scott was playing for the Red Sox, and while Boston was in Kansas City playing a series against the Royals at Royals Stadium, the two clubs made a trade sending Scott across the field to the Royals clubhouse in exchange for outfielder Tom Poquette.

The series began on Monday June 11, 1979, and Scott appeared in the first game, which the Red Sox won 4–0. Tom Poquette appeared in the Tuesday game as a pinch-hitter in the Royals 7–6 win. The trade happened before the Wednesday game, in which Scott did not play, but Poquette was 2-for-4 relieving center fielder Fred Lynn in an 11–3 Red Sox win.

Scott first appeared in a Royals uniform three days later in Milwaukee on Saturday, June 16, 1979, for one of the most memorable games in Royals history. The Brewers jumped out to a 6–0 lead after three innings and led 11–2 after four innings. At that point Royals manager Whitey Herzog took several of his starters out of the game including George Brett, Fred Patek, and Darrell Porter.

The Royals trailed 11–6 in the top of the ninth inning when they struck for eight runs. George Scott started at first base for the Royals and went 2-for-5 at the plate. His second hit was a two-run single that started the Royals' eight-run onslaught in the top of the ninth that resulted in their wild come-from-behind 14–11 victory at County Stadium.

And by virtue of his jersey, George Scott put himself into the Royals all-time record book. He took the field that day as the first-ever Royals player to have donned the number 0. The Royals released Scott on August 17, 1979, so his stay was brief—almost nonexistent, just like the number he wore.

13. 475 feet.

And I'll give you two guesses at who hit the ball, and the second one doesn't count. The great Buck O'Neil was known for many things, but one of them was his baseball wisdom earned over decades around the game at all levels. Buck was blessed to be around to see almost everything, and he would tell you that one of the greatest things about baseball is that you could be around forever and not really see it all. The game can surprise and delight you at any time (along with humbling you and leaving you wanting to curse it at times as well).

One of the surprises and delights for Buck was a singular sound he heard in 1986. It was a particular sound of the bat hitting a baseball. Not the normal crack of the bat that is familiar and comforting every spring. Buck claimed this was a very distinctive sound—one he had heard only two times before, but had remembered it all the same. "I heard it again."

He explained the first time he had heard this sound was as a kid in his home state of Florida. He heard it standing outside the fence of a ballpark where the Yankees were playing an exhibition game. He said he climbed a tree to see inside the park and it was Babe Ruth taking batting practice. Years later when Buck was playing in the Negro Leagues he said he was in the clubhouse one day when he heard the sound again and raced out to see it was Josh Gibson.

Bo Jackson hit his first major-league home run on September 14, 1986. The 475-foot blast against Seattle's Mike Moore was the longest home run ever recorded at Royals/Kauffman Stadium.

In 1986, Buck was at Royals Stadium, as he was for almost every Royals game for many years, coming out of the Stadium Club when he heard that distinctive sound once again. He looked to the field and at the plate for batting practice was none other than Bo Jackson.

As you should have guessed, if you didn't know, Bo Jackson hit the longest home run ever at Royals/Kauffman Stadium according to the Royals record book. I say according to the Royals record book because home-run distances are by their nature an inexact measurement. Some believe Johnny Bench's 1973 All-Star Game home run was longer. Maybe, but there is no record.

A Mike Trout home run at Kauffman Stadium a few years ago was measured at a longer distance than Bo's blast, but the current system projects where a ball would have landed if it reached level ground again even with the batter with no obstacles or impediments. It is meant to be more precise, but is itself empirical to some degree. So, the longest home run in Royals/Kauffman Stadium continues to be the first career blast by Bo Jackson on a Sunday afternoon, September 14, 1986.

The Royals were already staked to a 3–0 lead when Bo Jackson led off the bottom of the fourth inning against Mariners starter Mike Moore. Jackson launched a Moore fastball up near the light standards beyond the wall in left-center field near the top of the grass terrace that was then part of the ballpark. In Kauffman Stadium's 2016 configuration, it would be somewhere near the fountain bar near the statue of Mr. and Mrs. Kauffman on the left field side of the Outfield Experience. It was a blast.

The Jackson home run started a five-run Royals fourth inning that extended their lead to 8–0, on the way to a 10–3 win over Seattle. Every Royals starter had at least one hit in the game, with DH Jorge Orta leading the way with three hits and four RBIs including a two-out, two-run homer following Bo in that same fourth inning. Still that game will always be remembered for the Bo home run alone—his first career home run that traveled an estimated 475 feet, the longest in Royals/Kauffman Stadium history.

14. Harold Reynolds.

Some of the things Bo Jackson did on the field seemed preposterous. When some of his exploits are discussed years later, they seem like tall tales full of hyperbole. But many of them were just as hard to believe at the time, even if you were privileged to see them with your own eyes. One case in point would be "The Throw" in Seattle.

On June 5, 1989, the Royals were on the road playing the Mariners at the Kingdome. The Royals scored one run in the top of the first and two runs in the top of the second against Brian Holman. Royals starter Floyd Bannister had the Mariners shut out through seven innings, but Seattle rallied for two runs in the bottom of the eighth—and, one strike away from a Royals win, Jay Buhner tied the game with a two-out solo homer in the bottom of the ninth against Steve Farr.

All of that was just stage setting for one of the most memorable plays in Royals history. The Mariners' Harold Reynolds singled with one out in the bottom of the 10th inning. Then Scott Bradley followed with a double tracked down by Bo Jackson on the warning track in deep left field. Jackson wheeled and fired the ball from the wall to home plate on a line to get Reynolds at the plate with the potential game-winning run. The ball traveled from Jackson's hand to Bob Boone's catcher's mitt and never touched the ground. Play-by-play announcer Denny Matthews called it a "trolley wire" throw; others called it a missile.

"The Throw" was stunning to all, not least of which to Harold Reynolds. A fast runner by any measure, Reynolds led the American League in stolen bases with 60 in 1987. He led the American league in triples with 11 in 1988. He wasn't slow in 1989, but he wasn't fast enough to outrun the speeding bullet thrown by Bo Jackson. For Bo it wasn't much. He said of the play, "I just caught the ball and threw. End of story. It's nothing to brag about. Don't make a big issue out of it."

There was plenty to brag about even if he didn't, and it also wasn't the end of the story. The Royals began the top of the 13th inning with three consecutive singles from Danny Tartabull, Bill Buckner, and the third from Matt Winters, which plated Tartabull with the go-ahead run. With one out, an RBI single by Mike Macfarlane provided the Royals an insurance run and they defeated the Mariners 5–3.

The RBI for Winters was the first of his major-league career, on just his second major-league hit. The 29-year-old had finally made the big leagues after playing 11 seasons and a total of 1,289 minor-league games. Winters's major-league career consisted of 42 games with the 1989 Royals in which he hit .234 with two home runs and nine RBIs, but that first RBI was the winning run in one of the most memorable games in Royals history.

15. Mike Moustakas.

Mike Moustakas made his big-league debut wearing number 8 for the Royals. He wore number 8 for the Royals in the 2014 World Series. He wore number 8 for the Royals in the 2015 MLB All-Star Game. He wore number 8 when he turned a double play to end Game 4 of the 2015 World Series. But on September 12, 2015, he went into the Royals record book with the number 9.

Prior to that date, 12 players shared the team record for most RBIs in a single game. The first was catcher Jerry Grote (June 3, 1981 vs. Seattle) and the most recent Billy Butler (April 7, 2013 at Philadelphia)—Bo Jackson had done it twice, because he is Bo Jackson and that is what Bo Jackson does. The others to drive in a lucky seven: Willie Aikens, George Brett, Frank White, Kevin Seitzer, Johnny Damon, Raul Ibanez, Mike Sweeney, and Jose Guillen.

Moustakas would best them all. Entering the top of the sixth that Saturday afternoon in Baltimore, the Royals trailed the Orioles 4–1 and Moustakas was 0-for-2. That would soon change, as the Royals scored five runs that inning, including a Moustakas two-run single to take a 6–4 lead.

In the seventh, Moustakas closed out another five-run outburst by the Royals, hitting his second career grand slam home run. The Royals led 11–7 and Moustakas had six RBIs—but neither tally was finished. Eric Hosmer reached with a one-out walk in the top of the ninth, and Kendrys Morales followed with a double. Which brought Moustakas to the plate with a chance to make Royals history, and he promptly did by launching a three-run home run.

Through five innings the Royals had a single run, and Mike Moustakas was 0-for-2 with a strikeout and a pop fly. Through nine innings the Royals had a 14–6 win over the Orioles at Camden Yards, and Mike Moustakas was 3-for-5 with two home runs and a Royals club record of nine RBIs in a single game all to himself.

16. Amos Otis.

The Royals have had some top-quality base stealers, from Fred Patek and Willie Wilson to Jarrod Dyson and Terrance Gore. During Carlos Beltran's Royals career, his success rate of stealing bases was the best in baseball history—that's everyone ever in the history of the game, at least those with 100 or more steals, and in this case anything less wasn't worthy of note.

But none of them, and none of the others not mentioned (Bo Jackson, Brian McRae, Vince Coleman, Tom Goodwin . . . just to name a few more) have topped what Amos Otis did on Tuesday, September 7, 1971.

The Royals were hosting the Milwaukee Brewers at Municipal Stadium, and Otis started his game with a two-out single in the bottom of the first inning. He stole second, but was left stranded when Gail Hopkins grounded out to end the inning. Otis singled again leading off the bottom of the fourth. He then stole second again, moved to third on a groundout by Hopkins, and scored on a sacrifice fly by Bob Oliver to tie the game at 1–1.

After Sandy Valdespino's two-out RBI double scored Fred Patek to put the Royals in front 2–1 in the bottom of the fifth, Otis singled for a third time and immediately stole second for the third time as well. With the game tied 3–3 in the bottom of the seventh, Otis almost single-handedly, or perhaps single-footedly, put the Royals back in front.

With two outs and nobody on base, Otis singled for the fourth time in the contest. Just as before, he immediately stole second base for the fourth time. Then Otis decided to set sail for third and made it safely with his fifth stolen base of the game. Brewers catcher and future Royals teammate Darrell Porter threw wildly to third allowing Otis to score the go-ahead run.

Otis was 4-for-4 with two runs scored and a Royals single-game record of five stolen bases—and the Royals needed them all to defeat the Brewers 4–3. It was the first time a major-league player had recorded five steals in one game since Johnny Nuen of the Detroit Tigers on July 9, 1927.

17. Ferguson Jenkins.

George Brett made his major-league debut on August 2, 1973 and got his first base hit that very night. He would play 13 games for the Royals in 1973—four in August and nine more in September—hitting .125 (5-for-40) with no home runs or RBIs. He did hit two doubles and scored twice, but the big numbers and highlights would have to wait.

One of those highlights came four days after George was recalled from Omaha for good the following season. The Royals were in Arlington playing the Rangers on Wednesday May 8, 1974, and manager Jack McKeon had his rookie third baseman hitting ninth in the Royals' batting order against veteran right-handed pitcher Ferguson Jenkins.

In Brett's first at-bat of the game he laced a two-out double in the top of the second, but was stranded when Fred Patek grounded out to end the inning. Hal McRae put the Royals in front with an RBI single in the third. Brett was out on a fly ball to center field in his second at-bat, which ended the top of the fourth.

Jenkins was still on the mound in the top of the seventh trailing 1–0 in a pitchers' battle with Royals starter Al Fitzmorris. With two outs and the bases empty, George Brett came to the plate for his third at-bat and launched a long fly to right-center field for his first big-league home run to give the Royals a 2–0 advantage.

Home runs were big in the game as Fitzmorris surrendered a two-run shot to Mike Hargrove in the bottom of the seventh that tied the game. But John Mayberry returned the favor with a two-run home run off Jenkins in the top of the eighth, which turned out to be the decisive blow in the Royals 4–2 win.

Brett's first career home run was one of two he would hit off fellow National Baseball Hall of Famer Ferguson Jenkins. He was the first of 211 pitchers George would hit home runs against during his career. It was also the first of 21 home runs George would hit at Arlington Stadium—the second most he hit at any single road ballpark (he hit 22 at Tiger Stadium).

18. 317.

George Brett had 317 home runs in his career—a Royals record. The final home run of his career came on September 26, 1993 at Kauffman Stadium, and in typical George Brett fashion, it was both meaningful and unforgettable.

Only one day earlier, George Brett had announced his retirement, effective in a precious few days with only eight games to go in the 1993 season. However, it also set the stage for a healthy dose of Brett dramatics and a memorable game to cap off a memorable career.

The story started in the bottom of the first inning, when Angels starter John Farrell walked Felix Jose with one out. Jose immediately stole second and scored on a George Brett RBI single to put the Royals ahead 1–0. You could feel that maybe George would be authoring a thrilling final chapter to his storied career.

With the Royals down 3–1, Brent Mayne singled with one out in the bottom of the fourth. Jose Lind followed with a single, and Kevin Koslofski walked to load the bases. Felix Jose's sacrifice fly scored Mayne to make it 3–2 Angels. Then right on cue, George Brett launched a three-run homer to put the Royals back in front 5–3. It was career home run #316 for Brett. The lead didn't last.

The Angels were ahead 8–5 into the bottom of the ninth. With one out and nobody on base, Angels pitcher Steve Frey hit George Brett, and it seemed that maybe magically it could start a Royals rally to keep the story going. It did. Three consecutive two-out walks and a two-RBI single by Mike Macfarlane somehow got the game tied and into extra innings. How would the story end? Really, do you even need to ask?

With two outs in the bottom of the 10th, guess who came to bat? Yes, it was exactly the guy you would think to dramatically end the story. He launched a solo homer against Pat Swingle of the Angels and the Royals had a walk-off 9–8 win. It was the 317th and final career home run for George Brett.

So raucous was the home crowd that Brett was moved to come out of the clubhouse, return to the field, and acknowledge the fans. "When you get ovations like that, it makes you feel so good inside," Brett said at the time. "I'm not the player I once was, and I'll be the first to say that, but they still appreciate the effort and they still appreciate the success that I've had." As for the home-run ball? "I'll take it home," said Brett, who added, "if it's my last one." It was the last one, and it was a walkoff winner.

19. Six.

There have been six pitchers to win 100 or more games in a Kansas City Royals uniform, and all of them are members of the Royals Hall of Fame. The first to reach the milestone was Paul Splittorff with his 100th win on July 21, 1978.

Three of the stalwarts of the Royals rotation in the late 1970s and early 1980s are all members of the Royals 100 Win Club with Splittorff, Dennis Leonard, and Larry Gura, and it seems all but certain that Steve Busby would have been a fourth if injuries had not curtailed his career. Busby had 59 wins through his first three full major-league seasons (1972–1975).

Busby would only record 11 more wins over the last five years of his career (1976–1980) as he battled shoulder injuries. It's amazing to look back and realize that the Royals won four division titles in five years from 1976 through 1980—all after losing perhaps their best starting pitcher.

But even had Busby been healthy, Dennis Leonard would have been right there battling him for the number-one starter role. No right-hander in all of baseball won more games than Leonard did from 1975 to 1981. He was a workhorse, compiling 120 wins in that span, with only Steve Carlton posting more victories during that time period. The Royals would also lose him to injury during the 1983 season.

Without injury, it is conceivable that both Leonard and Busby could have still been in the Royals rotation in 1985 when they finally won the World Series. Leonard only pitched briefly in 1985 during his long, arduous return from his 1983 knee injury—it was his age 34 season. Busby retired following the 1980 season after multiple comeback attempts from shoulder injuries; he was 35 years old in 1985.

Larry Gura was the crafty left-hander who helped the Royals maintain a strong three-man rotation after the loss of Busby. Gura pitched mostly out of the bullpen in his first two years with the Royals (1976 and 1977), before moving into the rotation in 1978. He then rattled off seven consecutive seasons with double-digit wins, including two 18-win campaigns (1980 and 1982).

There were a few months of the 1984 season in which the Royals pitching staff included five of the six pitchers who have won 100 or more games in a Royals uniform. Leonard was working back from injury that season, but Splittorff and Gura were still members of the starting rotation when the season began. They were joined on Opening Day by two rookies named Bret Saberhagen and Mark Gubicza.

If Royals starting pitching were a relay race, Saberhagen and Gubicza were perfectly placed (along with Danny Jackson) to take the baton and continue the Royals run of championship baseball. And that is exactly what they did. They both won

10 games in their rookie season of 1984, the same season the Royals returned to postseason play by winning their first division title since 1980.

Then, of course, they were both key members of the 1985 world champions when starting pitching was the key strength that drove the Royals to the title. It was a full turnover from the successful Royals starting rotation of the early 1980s—the baton was passed and advanced.

The most recent pitcher with 100 or more wins in a Royals uniform debuted in 1989 and became a standout in his rookie year of 1990. Kevin Appier won 12 games in that rookie season and proceeded to post double-digit victories in six of his first seven seasons. As Saberhagen and Gubicza took the baton from Splittorff, Gura, and Leonard, Appier played a similar role in keeping the tradition rolling—though he never had a consistent win-producing rotation-mate like his predecessors.

Hopefully there will be more members of the Royals 100 Win Club to emerge from this generation of championship Royals. The original six all played important roles in keeping the Royals competitive for many seasons, and a few new members to the club would certainly help do the same.

20. Mike Fiore.

The Royals acquired Michael Gary Joseph Fiore from the Baltimore Orioles with the 17th pick in the Expansion Draft on October 15, 1968. He had made his major-league debut on September 21, 1968 and played six games for the Orioles. He did get his first career hit with the Orioles, but his first home run would have to wait until 1969.

Fiore made the 1969 Royals Opening Day roster as one of the inaugural 25 players. But he did not play in that first game of April 8, 1969, despite the fact it went 12 long innings. Still, he would put his name in the Royals' record book several days later in Oakland.

Outfielder/first baseman Mike Fiore hit the first home run in Royals history on April 13, 1969 in Game 1 of a doubleheader at Oakland. The second-inning leadoff home run against Blue Moon Odom came in the fifth game of the Royals' inaugural season.

Four games into the 1969 season and the Royals' record stood at 3–1 with two walkoff wins, but they still had not registered their first home run. That changed on Sunday, April 13, 1969, during the first game of a doubleheader against the Athletics in Oakland.

Mike Fiore led off the top of the second inning with a home run against Oakland starter Johnny Lee "Blue Moon" Odom to give the Royals a 1–0 lead—the first home run in Royals history. And it would be a good omen for a fourth victory in five tries.

Royals starter Bill Butler pitched the first 5 ⅓ innings allowing only one run on two hits. He was relieved by Moe Drabowsky, who did him one better by throwing the final 4 ⅔ innings allowing only two hits and no runs. The Royals emerged with a 4–1 win in Game 1 of the Sunday doubleheader at the Oakland-Alameda Coliseum—all ignited courtesy of Mike Fiore's first career home run, and the first home run in Royals franchise history.

Did You Know?—*The Howser Trophy—the annual award for college baseball's most outstanding player—is named after Royals Hall of Fame manager Dick Howser. The first recipient was Mike Fiore Jr. in 1987—the son of Mike Fiore Sr., who was a member of the inaugural 1969 Royals.*

21. John Wathan.

John Wathan has had one of the most interesting and varied careers in Royals franchise history. Few are more true blue than Wathan, who since he was drafted in 1971 through today, with only a brief interruption, has served the organization in nearly every capacity. Known simply as "Duke"—a nickname earned from his dead-on John Wayne impression—Wathan has been a key contributor as a player, coach, manager, broadcaster, and scout. Those who devote an entire career to the game are often referred to as "good baseball men." John Wathan is that and more.

It all started when he was the club's first-round selection (fourth overall) in the 1971 January draft out of the University of San Diego. His versatility made him a manager's favorite and helped him reach the big leagues by 1976. The Royals made their first postseason in his rookie year and won a world championship in his last—all the while Wathan was a steady and dependable presence behind the plate, at first base, and in the outfield.

Even with all that, the all-time major-league record he broke and still holds (through 2016) might be the coolest factoid about his Royals career. Conventional wisdom says catchers do not steal bases. Stealing bases requires speed, right? And catchers are slow, right? Don't tell John Wathan that. Those would be fighting words.

Wathan was a very notable exception to that conventional wisdom. He posted 17 stolen bases in 1980 and 11 more in 1981, but not all of those came as a catcher. In 1982 he became the Royals regular starting catcher and proceeded to run down a major-league record. And even more impressive, he had to overcome a fractured ankle suffered on July 5th of that season.

The major-league record for stolen bases by a catcher was 30 posted by Hall of Famer Ray Schalk in 1916. Wathan already had a career high with 26 stolen bases when the injury occurred. He missed five weeks and it looked like Schalk's record was safe. It wasn't.

Wathan returned on August 10th and two weeks later had run his stolen base total to a record-tying 30. On August 24 in Arlington, Texas, the Royals led 3–2 when Wathan led off the top of the seventh inning with a single. Greg Pryor moved him to second with a sacrifice bunt, then Wathan took off for third. Jim Sundberg's throw was late and umpire Bill Haller called Wathan safe—he had the record.

The Royals went on to defeat the Rangers 5–3. Wathan went on to swipe six more bases as a catcher in 1982 and re-set the record, now all his own, at three dozen steals in a single season by a catcher. No backstop has caught him since.

22. John Mayberry.

There are many home-run questions in Royals history with the answer being John Mayberry. Big John came to the Royals on December 2, 1971 from the Houston Astros in exchange for pitchers Lance Clemons and Jim York. After being the Astros' first-round selection in the 1967 June draft, Mayberry had posted a couple of minor-league seasons with 20+ home runs.

One of those seasons was 1969, when he blasted 21 home runs for the Oklahoma City 89ers of the American

On August 24, 1982, John Wathan broke National Baseball Hall of Famer Ray Schalk's record of 30 stolen bases by a catcher in a single season. The record-breaker came when Wathan stole third base in a 5–3 victory over the Rangers in Arlington, Texas.

Association. Some of those came against the 1969 American Association Champion Omaha Royals, and the Royals organization took notice. The Royals needed a power hitter and they got one in Mayberry.

In his first season in Kansas City, Mayberry slugged 25 home runs and posted 100 RBIs. He also hit .298 and was named the 1972 Royals Player of the Year. It was his 25th and final home run of that 1972 season that went down in Kansas City baseball history.

The date was Friday, September 29, 1972, and the Royals were facing off against the Oakland Athletics at Kansas City's Municipal Stadium. Mayberry had tied the game at 2–2 with

Royals Hall of Famer John Mayberry hitting the first home run at Royals Stadium on April 10, 1973. The fifth-inning two-run shot against Bob Gogolewski was the only home run during the Royals' 12–1 win over the Rangers in the ballpark's inaugural game.

an RBI triple scoring Richie Scheinblum in the bottom of the fourth inning off 1971 American League Cy Young Winner and Most Valuable Player Vida Blue. Mayberry would give the Royals the lead in the fifth inning with a two-out three-run home run. The blast powered the Royals to a 9–3 win and was the last home run by a member of the home team at the ballpark at 22nd and Brooklyn.

Fast forward to Opening Night the following year on April 10, 1973, the debut game for Kansas City's new ballpark christened Royals Stadium. The Royals ambushed Texas on that cold Tuesday night in Kansas City, scoring four runs in the bottom of the first—then four more in the bottom of the fourth. Again it was Mayberry who would make some more Royals history in the bottom of the fifth.

With two outs and the bases empty, Amos Otis singled off Rangers reliever Bob Gogolewski and John Mayberry followed with a blast deep into what would become the Water Spectacular beyond the right field wall. The two-run shot was the first home run ever at Royals Stadium and expanded the Royals lead to 8–0 on their way to a blowout 12–1 win over the Rangers. Mayberry's fellow Royals Hall of Famer Paul Splittorff had the good fortune to be pitching on both occasions and picked up the win in both games.

Did You Know?—*Tiger Stadium was the first major-league ballpark to surrender 10,000 home runs. The 9,997th, 9,998th, and 10,000th were all hit by Royals in a 12–6 victory on July 22, 1993—the milestone a two-run ninth-inning shot off the bat of shortstop Greg Gagne.*

23. Raul Ibanez.

Raul Ibanez is an interesting character in Royals history. Perhaps most notably, he had two different stints with the

Royals, the first from 2001 through 2003 and the second more than a full decade later in the stretch run of the 2014 season. He made an impact in both instances.

He first came to the Royals as a free agent from the Seattle Mariners organization on January 22, 2001. At the time he was a 29-year-old outfielder without much of a big-league track record. He had played in 231 games over the course of the previous five seasons in Seattle with 14 home runs and 58 RBIs. Ibanez was a non-roster invitee to spring training that season and worked his way onto the Opening Day roster.

In 2001 alone he hit 13 home runs and recorded 54 RBIs for the Royals. All of that came in a season in which the Royals designated him for assignment not once, but twice. He could have been claimed by any team, but cleared waivers both times. Then came 2002.

At age 30, the struggles of 10 seasons in professional baseball all seemed to make sense as his perseverance was rewarded. He thrived as a regular for the Royals, playing in 137 games and hitting .294 with 24 home runs and 103 RBIs. He was good again the following year with the surprising 2003 Royals, hitting .294 with 18 home runs and 90 RBIs in 157 games.

Success was far from overnight for Ibanez, but success is what Ibanez had earned. He also earned a free agent contract back with the Seattle Mariners. The late bloomer had a 19-year career that included being named to the 2009 National League All-Star team, the same year he was part of the National League Champion Philadelphia Phillies.

From a Royals perspective the Raul Ibanez story came full circle in 2014, when after being released by the Angels he signed with the Royals on June 30 and joined a completely different generation of Royals as a veteran presence.

On July 2, 2014, the second game in his second stint with the Royals, Raul Ibanez hit an eighth-inning solo home run for the Royals' third run in a 4–0 win at Target Field in Minneapolis. At 42 years and 32 days old, Ibanez became the oldest player to ever hit a home run for the Royals, besting Hal McRae, who held the previous Father Time record at 41 years and 296 days old on May 2, 1987 in a 5–4 Royals win over Cleveland at Royals Stadium.

Ibanez would extend his record with a fifth-inning solo shot at Oakland on August 1, 2014. It was the only run the Royals scored in the game, and the only run they needed in a 1–0 win over the A's. He was 42 years and 62 days old. During his second go-round with the Royals, Ibanez hit only .188 with those two home runs and five RBIs, but his impact was immeasurable anyway.

The 2014 Royals had lost four consecutive games coming out of the All-Star break and fell two games under .500 at 48-50. Before their game in Chicago on Tuesday, July 22, Ibanez spoke at a rare players only meeting and stressed to his young teammates the feeling that he assured them other teams had about the Royals. He told them other teams thought the Royals could and should be a contender and that they should believe the same about themselves.

That night the Royals posted a 7–1 win over the White Sox at U.S. Cellular Field. The win sparked a 41-23 run that would lead to the 2014 Royals ending a 29-year playoff drought.

24. Clint Hurdle.

Clinton Merrick Hurdle was the Royals' first-round selection (ninth overall) in the 1975 June draft out of Merritt Island High School in Merritt Island, Florida. He would quickly become one of the most talked about minor-league players in Royals history.

Clint Hurdle was so much of a star in the making that he was only the second Royals player to ever appear on the cover of *Sports Illustrated*. The first was George Brett on the June 21, 1976 issue, but Brett was in his second big-league season and racing toward his first batting title. The Hurdle cover issue was March 20, 1978, after he had only played nine big-league games the previous season. The headline captured the moment— "'This Year's Phenom' Kansas City's Clint Hurdle."

Hurdle made the jump from Class-A ball in 1976, all the way to Triple-A Omaha in 1977 where he would win American

Clint Hurdle is the youngest Royals player to hit a home run at 20 years and 50 days old. The two-run home run in his major-league debut against Glenn Abbott on September 18, 1977 started the Royals' scoring in an 8–3 win over Seattle at Royals Stadium.

Association Most Valuable Player honors, hitting .328 with 16 home runs and 66 RBIs. The Royals called him up to the big leagues after the Omaha season ended, and he made his major-league debut on September 18, 1977 in Kansas City.

At the time of his debut, Hurdle was the youngest player to ever appear with the Royals, clocking in at 20 years and 50 days old. Batting in the fifth spot in Manager Whitey Herzog's lineup, he grounded out in his first at-bat against Seattle starter Glenn Abbott. But he made his presence felt in his second time up in the bottom of the fifth inning.

John Mayberry led off with a double, then Hurdle smashed a two-run home run for his first major-league hit, run, and RBI all in one swing. The blast also started a four-run inning for the Royals on their way to an 8–3 win over the Mariners at Royals Stadium.

Hurdle has since slipped from his rank as the youngest Royals player ever. But he remains the youngest Royals player to ever hit a home run, and he led the Royals to a win in his debut game. Hurdle played five years for the Royals with some success. His best year came in the Royals' 1980 American League Championship season when he hit .294 with 10 home runs and 60 RBIs.

Yet the superstardom his *Sports Illustrated* cover fanfare anticipated never quite materialized. The Royals traded him to the Cincinnati Reds on December 11, 1981 in exchange for right-handed pitcher Scott Brown, who pitched 14 games for the 1983 Omaha Royals, then never again.

Hurdle would play five more big-league seasons with the Cincinnati Reds, New York Mets, and St. Louis Cardinals. But he found greater success as a coach and manager, including back in the big leagues where he led the 2007 Colorado Rockies to their first-ever National League Championship.

25. Two.

Through the 2016 season, the Royals have twice led the American League in wins. The first was a great season that ended in heartbreak. The second was a great season that ended with the largest parade in Kansas City history.

The 1977 Royals had one of the great second-half runs of any team in the history of baseball. When play began on August 17, 1977, the Royals stood with a record of 64-51 in fourth place and two games behind the division-leading Minnesota Twins. On that evening the Royals won 5–3 at Municipal Stadium in Cleveland beginning a 10-game winning streak—the first double-digit streak in franchise history.

The 10-game winning streak was just the start of an incredible stretch in which the Royals would win 35 of 39 games through September 15, 1977. They went from 64-51 and two games out of first place, to 91-54 and 10 ½ games ahead in first place all by themselves. The 1977 American League Western Division Champion Royals finished the season with a 102-60 record, two games better than the American League Eastern Division Champion New York Yankees.

However, the Yankees would finish one game better than the Royals, defeating Kansas City three games to two in the 1977 American League Championship Series. The Royals lost the fifth and deciding game at home, falling to the Yankees 5–3 after going to the ninth inning with a 3–2 lead at Royals Stadium.

The 2015 Royals simply had one of the best seasons in franchise history. They started the campaign with a seven-game winning streak to set the tone of things to come. They were 52-34 at the All-Star break, 4 ½ games in front of the second-place Minnesota Twins in the American League Central. They also had four more wins than either the Eastern Division–leading New York Yankees or the Western Division–leading Los Angeles Angels.

The 2015 Royals' high-water mark in the regular season came on September 3 when they stood 82-51, 13 games in front of the second-place Minnesota Twins in the American League Central. They also had six more wins than the AL East–leading Toronto Blue Jays, who had the second most victories in the league.

The hard-charging Blue Jays (91-65) actually passed the Royals (90-66) for the best record in the American League on Monday, September 28 with six games remaining in the season. The Royals then ended the regular season on a five-game winning streak to finish with a 95-67 record, two games better than the Eastern Division champion–Toronto Blue Jays at 93-69.

Those two games gave the Royals home field advantage during the playoffs, which they took advantage of winning the deciding Game 5 of the ALDS against Houston at Kauffman Stadium. They then won their second consecutive American League pennant in six games over the Blue Jays, with three wins coming at home, including the clinching victory in Game 6 of the ALCS.

It was the 2015 American League All-Star Game victory that gave the Royals home field advantage in the 2015 World Series. In that series it may seem home field advantage was less decisive as the Royals won in five games over the Mets—though you couldn't tell that to anyone who lived through the Royals' 14-inning win at home in Game 1. There's no place like home, there's no place like home.

LATE INNINGS

ALL-STAR LEVEL

1. Bret Saberhagen, David Cone, and Zack Greinke all won Cy Young Awards with the Royals. What made the Cy Young Awards won by Saberhagen, Cone, and Greinke a first in Major League Baseball history? *Answer on page 95.*

2. What special first in Major League Baseball history was the 2015 World Series matchup between the New York Mets and Kansas City Royals? *Answer on page 96.*

3. How many players have recorded a six-hit game with the Royals? *Answer on page 99.*

4. What is the most runs the Royals scored in a single game? *Answer on page 101.*

5. Who was the first Royal to win a Gold Glove? *Answer on page 102.*

6. What was the first major-league trade in Royals history? *Answer on page 103.*

7. Who was the Royals' first regular-season opponent in 1969? *Answer on page 104.*

8. Royals/Kauffman Stadium has hosted two MLB All-Star Games. What Royals players appeared as American League All-Stars in those two Midsummer Classics? *Answer on page 106.*

9. Reliability and dependability are important in baseball—as in life. Through the 2016 season, how many players in Royals history have played in every regular-season game of a single season? *Answer on page 108.*

10. Name the three father/son combinations to play for the Royals. *Answer on page 110.*

11. Three Royals pitchers have thrown no-hitters. Can you name them? *Answer on page 112.*

12. What Les Milgram Royals Player of the Year Award winner was acquired by Kansas City in a one-dollar waiver wire transaction? *Answer on page 116.*

13. Who holds the Royals record for consecutive games played? *Answer on page 119.*

14. Who is the only player to have a three home run game for the Royals at home? *Answer on page 120.*

15. What is the most number of games over .500 the Royals have been during any season in club history? *Answer on page 121.*

16. Denny Matthews has called Royals games on the radio from their first game in 1969 and has earned the title "Voice of the Royals," but he was the junior partner on the original Royals broadcast team. Who was the original "Voice of the Royals"? *Answer on page 122.*

17. What is the longest game by number of innings played in Royals history? *Answer on page 125.*

18. Who holds the Royals record for consecutive games with a home run? *Answer on page 128.*

19. Mike Sweeney is second on the Royals' all-time home run list with 197. How many home runs did Mike Sweeney hit *against* the Royals in his MLB career? *Answer on page 129.*

20. What Royals hurler once tied the American League record for most consecutive strikeouts by a pitcher in a single game? *Answer on page 131.*

21. Which Royals manager was the first in club history to win the American League Manager of the Year Award? *Answer on page 132.*

22. Who is the only manager to have had two separate stints leading the Royals? *Answer on page 133.*

23. Who was the first player to ever hit for the cycle with the Royals? *Answer on page 135.*

24. Which players have hit for the cycle twice with the Royals? *Answer on page 136.*

25. What major-league first do the Royals Dan Quisenberry and Jamie Quirk share? *Answer on page 139.*

ALL-STAR LEVEL —
ANSWERS

1. Zack Greinke's 2009 season with the Royals was one for the record books, and it resulted in the fourth Cy Young Award for a Royals pitcher. He extended the Royals line of Cy Young pitchers that started with Bret Saberhagen, who won the honor in both 1985 and 1989, and continued with Kansas City native David Cone who literally brought the award home in 1994. But Zack's 2009 Cy Young nod also made the Royals Major League Baseball's most successful Cy Young drafting organization—a fact that almost went without mention.

Look at the three names and consider their careers, and you'll see that the Kansas City Royals became the *first* Major League Baseball Club to have three of their own draft picks win Cy Young Awards while pitching for their original drafting organization.

There were other clubs that had two or one. But the Royals stood alone as the first organization with three *self-drafted* Cy Young Award winners. Let's look at some history.

The Cy Young was first awarded following the 1956 season and at first was given to the best pitcher in all of MLB—combining both the National and American Leagues. That changed in 1967 when the decision was made to recognize one pitcher from each league. From 1956 through 2009, 67 different pitchers had captured Cy Young honors, but only 36 won the award with their original club—a distinction all three Royals shared.

At the time Dodgers fans might have argued that they still led the way with six "self-developed" Cy Young Award winners, but the first three of those (Don Newcombe in 1956, Don Drysdale in 1962 and Sandy Koufax in 1963, 1965, and 1966) pre-dated baseball's amateur draft, which began in 1965. Three other Dodger-developed pitchers won the Cy Young Award for Los Angeles (Fernando Valenzuela 1981, Orel Hershiser 1988, and Eric Gagne 2003), but only one—Orel Hershiser—was acquired through the draft.

The A's also had three "self-developed" Cy Young winners (Vida Blue 1971, Catfish Hunter 1974, and Barry Zito 2002). But Hunter's signing also pre-dated the draft—he was acquired as an amateur free agent by the Kansas City Athletics in 1964. All of which made the Royals the first organization to have *drafted* three of their own eventual Cy Young hurlers.

Saberhagen, Cone, and Greinke put the Royals in a league of their own.

2. There were many things about the 2015 World Series that made it special—especially from a Kansas City Royals perspective, first among them the final result. But the matchup between the New York Mets and the Royals made it a historic Fall Classic before the first pitch was thrown by Edinson Volquez at 7:07 p.m. on Tuesday, October 27, 2015 at Kauffman Stadium.

The expansion era of Major League Baseball began in 1961 when, for the first time since its inception in 1901, the American League added two new franchises—the Los Angeles Angels and the Washington Senators (who relocated and became the Texas Rangers in 1972). There had been relocations of teams over the decades, but this was the first instance of completely new franchises. The National League joined the expansion era in 1962 with the founding of the Houston Colt .45s (now the Houston Astros) and the New York Mets.

There have been four additional expansions in Major League Baseball since those first two. In 1969, the American League added the Kansas City Royals and the Seattle Pilots (who relocated and became the Milwaukee Brewers in 1970) while the National League added the San Diego Padres and the Montreal Expos (who relocated and became the Washington Nationals in 2005). The American League added the Seattle Mariners and the Toronto Blue Jays in 1977. The National League welcomed the Colorado Rockies and the Florida Marlins in 1993. Each league added another franchise in 1998 with the Arizona Diamondbacks joining the National League and the Tampa Bay Devil Rays coming to the American League.

Fourteen franchises in all have been added to Major League Baseball since the start of the expansion era, and 12 of them have reached the World Series. The only expansion franchises not to have won a league pennant through the 2016 season are the Montreal Expos/Washington Nationals and the Seattle Mariners.

The first National League expansion franchise to reach the World Series was the New York Mets when they won the 1969 Fall Classic against the Baltimore Orioles. The first American League expansion franchise to reach the World Series was the Kansas City Royals in 1980, but they lost to the Philadelphia Phillies. The Royals did become the first American League expansion franchise to win the World Series when they returned in 1985 and defeated the St. Louis Cardinals.

Although the Mets and Royals were the first from each league, other expansion clubs have since reached and won the World Series. The Texas Rangers played in back-to-back World Series in 2010 and 2011 against the Giants and Cardinals. The

Angels reached and won the World Series against the Giants in 2002. The Houston Astros made it to the World Series in 2005 against the Chicago White Sox. The Milwaukee Brewers played the St. Louis Cardinals in the 1982 World Series. The San Diego Padres played in the World Series in 1984 against the Tigers and in 1998 against the Yankees. The Blue Jays won the 1992 World Series over the Atlanta Braves and the 1993 World Series against the Phillies. The Rockies reached the 2007 World Series to play the Red Sox. The Marlins won the World Series against Cleveland in 1997 and again over the Yankees in 2003. The Diamondbacks won the 2001 World Series defeating the Yankees, and the Rays reached the Fall Classic in 2008 against the Phillies. More than half a century after the expansion era started, expansion franchises reaching and winning the World Series has become commonplace and barely even of note anymore—but the 2015 World Series was a different twist on what seemed an old story.

In 2015 two expansion franchises faced off against each other in the Fall Classic for the first time. Seems hard to believe,

Kauffman Stadium hosted Game 1 of the 2015 World Series, featuring the New York Mets against the Kansas City Royals. It was the first World Series game to ever match two expansion franchises (October 27, 2015).

doesn't it? But it's true, the very first World Series between National League and American League expansion franchises came 54 years after the start of the expansion era.

And upon reflection it seemed fitting that it would be the Mets and Royals to make that bit of Major League Baseball history. The two were not only the expansion franchises that were the first from their leagues to reach and win the World Series, but also the two expansion franchises that had reached the Fall Classic the most times. The 2015 World Series was the fifth appearance by the New York Mets and the fourth for the Kansas City Royals.

3. Three.

Ted Williams, regarded as one of the best hitters in baseball history—if not the best—once said, "The hardest thing to do in baseball is to hit a round ball with a round bat, squarely." Some will take it a step further and say that hitting a baseball may be the hardest task in sports. If a hitter fails to get a hit in 70 percent of his at-bats, he comes away with a .300 batting average and is rightly considered a huge success.

Now think of the odds of a player collecting six hits in a single nine-inning game. It's a rare feat—much less common than even the more celebrated no-hitter. Through the 2015 season, in the combined history of the National League (founded in 1876) and the American League (founded in 1901), there have been 294 no-hitters. During that same time span, a player has recorded six hits in a nine-inning game only 72 times.

The first Royals player to accomplish the feat was Bob Oliver in one of the individual accomplishments that highlighted the Royals' inaugural 1969 season. On May 4, 1969 in Anaheim, Oliver collected a second-inning single, fourth-inning leadoff double, fifth-inning two-run home run, seventh-inning lead-off single, another RBI single later in that frame, then finished with a ninth-inning single.

He became the 20th player in American League history and the first since 1962 to collect six hits in a nine-inning game. Originally his fifth hit (his second in the seventh inning) was ruled an error on third baseman Aurelio Rodriguez, who threw the ball in the dirt on his throw to first base. It was later changed to a hit by the official scorer. Every Royals starter collected at least one hit and scored a run in the 15–1 win at Angel Stadium.

The 23rd player in American League history to hit safely six times in a game was the Royals' Kevin Seitzer during his rookie season. On Sunday, August 2, 1987 at Royals Stadium, Seitzer singled and scored the Royals' first run in the first inning, led off the bottom of the third with a home run, had an RBI single in the fourth, capped a four-run rally in the fifth with a three-run home run, singled again in the seventh, and finally capped his game off with a two-run ground-rule double in the eighth.

Seitzer did more than go 6-for-6 that afternoon when the

Rookie Kevin Seitzer had the first six-hit game ever at Royals Stadium on August 2, 1987. He went 6-for-6 against the Boston Red Sox in a 13–5 victory.

Royals defeated the Red Sox 13–5—the first six-hit game ever at Royals Stadium. It was also the first multi-homer game of his career, and the only one he would have with the Royals. He also tied the then Royals club record with seven RBIs in the game.

The third Royals player with six hits in a nine-inning game was Joe Randa on September 9, 2004 at Comerica Park in Detroit. Randa started with a two-RBI double in the Royals' four-run top of the first. He got the Royals 11-run top of the third started with a one-out single, then singled again for the Royals' seventh of 10 hits in the third. He singled in the fourth, led off the Royals' five-run sixth with a single, struck out in the seventh, then singled one last time in the ninth and scored his sixth run of the game. Randa was the first player in American League history to have six hits and score six runs in a single nine-inning game.

Since the Royals' founding in 1969, the Pittsburgh Pirates are the only other MLB franchise to record three six-hit games.

4. 26.

In that same September 9, 2004 game in which Joe Randa was 6-for-7 *(see previous question)*, he wasn't the only Royals offense. The Royals scored four runs in the top of the first, then kept adding more runs, scoring in all but two innings. Every Royals starter had at least one hit and scored at least one run.

The Royals scored four runs in the top of the first, two in the second, then an 11-run outburst in the top of the third, just one run short of the Royals' single-inning record. During that inning, the Royals tied an American League record when they had 13 consecutive batters reach base.

They weren't done, of course. The Royals scored two more in the fourth, then five more in the sixth inning before plating single runs in the eighth and ninth for good measure. And the Royals did all that damage with only one home run among their 26 hits—also a Royals all-time single-game record.

Angel Berroa completed the Royals' five-run sixth inning with a three-run home run. Perhaps fittingly, it was that lone home run that broke the then Royals record for most runs scored in a single game of 23 (April 6, 1974 vs Minnesota at Royals Stadium). The Berroa home run scored run number 22, 23 and 24 for the Royals.

The 26–5 win over the Tigers at Comerica Park in Detroit was the largest-ever winning margin for the Royals at 21 runs. Ironically it was the first game of a doubleheader, and as the baseball gods would have it, the Tigers shut out the Royals 8–0 in the second game. The 26 runs were still enough to set the Royals record for most runs scored in a doubleheader, although they could have paced themselves better.

5. Amos Otis.

Although Frank White remains the Royals player most associated with Rawlings Gold Gloves, he was not the first Royals player to win the honor. That distinction goes to fellow Royals Hall of Famer Amos Otis, who won the award following the 1971 season.

In fact, Otis was the first, second, and third Royals player to win a Rawlings Gold Glove when he repeated as an American League winner in 1973 and 1974. The three Gold Gloves won by Otis bridged the years between Municipal Stadium and the debut of Royals Stadium in 1973.

Otis was almost perfectly suited for the vast expanse of outfield space at Royals Stadium and set a precedent for Royals outfielders winning Gold Glove honors. The field itself has made outfielders with great defensive skill an imperative. It calls for center fielders with speed and range to track down balls from gap to gap and athletic corner outfielders with strong arms to keep baserunners honest.

The Royals have been fortunate to have had some of the best at all three outfield positions. Baseball's symbol of defensive excellence is the Rawlings Gold Glove Award, and since 1969 five different Royals outfielders have won the award at least once—second most in the American League during the span. The tradition started with Amos Otis, but has since been followed by Al Cowens, Willie Wilson, Jermaine Dye, and Alex Gordon.

Did You Know?—Through the 2016 season, the Royals have turned six triple plays in club history. The Royals record in those six games is an astonishing 0-6.

6. The Royals made their first major-league trade on December 12, 1968—sending veteran pitcher Hoyt Wilhelm, a future National Baseball Hall of Fame member, to the California Angels for catchers Ed Kirkpatrick and Dennis Paepke.

They had acquired Wilhelm with their 25th pick in the Expansion Draft from the Chicago White Sox. The veteran pitcher was 46 years old at the time of the draft, by far the oldest of the new Royals. He had already appeared in 937 major-league games, but the trade meant he would never actually take the field for the Royals.

He did, however, pitch four more years in the big leagues, ending his career at age 49 with the Los Angeles Dodgers in 1972. He was the first pitcher in major-league history to appear in 1,000 games, finishing his career with 1,070 appearances over 21 years.

Paepke played 80 games for the Royals, including a dozen games for the inaugural 1969 Royals. He played 60 games in a Royals uniform in 1971, and played his final six big-league games with the 1974 Royals. An arm injury in 1974 ended his playing career.

Edgar Leon Kirkpatrick was nicknamed "Spanky" after the "Our Gang" character. He was a bonus baby of the pre-draft era, signing with the Los Angeles Angels right after his 1962 graduation from Glendora High School in greater Los Angeles. The Angels signed him for $20,000, and he made his major-league debut on September 13, 1962 against the Kansas City Athletics at Dodger Stadium. He was just 17 years old at the time.

Kirkpatrick appeared in 613 games with the Royals over five seasons through 1973. He hit .257 with 14 home runs and 49 RBIs for the Royals in their 1969 inaugural season. He had a career-best 18 home runs and 62 RBIs for the Royals in 1970. The Royals traded him to the Pirates on December 4, 1973 along with Kurt Bevacqua and Royals Academy graduate Winston Cole for pitcher Nelson Briles and infielder Fernando Gonzalez.

All in all, Kirkpatrick's career spanned 16 big-league seasons. He played for the Angels, Royals, Pirates, Rangers, and Brewers.

7. Minnesota Twins.

There was rain in the area the morning and early afternoon of Tuesday, April 8, 1969, but nothing that would slow down the return of Major League Baseball to Kansas City. In fact, with the Athletics' move to Oakland after the 1967 season, 1968 had been the first year in Kansas City without professional baseball dating back to the debut of the 1884 Kansas City Unions of the Union Association. No more waiting.

Baseball was back. The Royals were hosting the Minnesota Twins at Municipal Stadium with game time set for 2:30 p.m. Royals founder Ewing Kauffman addressed the crowd, surprisingly only recorded as 17,688, during the pregame festivities. Senator Stuart Symington (D-MO) threw out the ceremonial first pitch; then 24-year-old Royals starter Wally Bunker threw the game's first pitch, a ball high and inside to Twins leadoff hitter Ted Uhlaender.

Bunker retired Uhlaender on a fly ball to right fielder Bob Oliver, Rod Carew on a groundball to second baseman Jerry Adair, and Tony Oliva on a popout to third baseman Joe Foy. One, two, three, and the Royals came to the plate.

The Royals' leadoff hitter was Lou Piniella, and he wasted no time, swinging at the first pitch by Twins starter Tom Hall, pulling a curveball just inside the bag at third and up the left field line for a double. The very first pitch a Royals hitter ever saw, and Piniella ripped it for the first hit in franchise history. Jerry Adair followed by lining a 1-2 pitch past third baseman Harmon Killebrew and into left field to drive in Piniella with the first run in Royals history. Two batters into the game and the Royals led 1–0.

Twins left fielder Graig Nettles tied the game with a solo home run in the top of the second inning. The Twins took a 3–1 lead with two runs in the top of the sixth. The Royals put together a two-out rally in the bottom of the sixth. Royals catcher Ellie Rodriguez doubled with two outs and Jackie Hernandez reached on an error charged to Killebrew. Pinch-hitter Jim Campanis followed with an RBI single scoring Rodriguez, and then an RBI single by Piniella scored Hernandez to tie the game 3–3.

The game went into extra innings. In the bottom of the 12th, Joe Foy singled with one out and advanced to second on a passed ball charged to Twins catcher Johnny Roseboro. The Twins intentionally walked Chuck Harrison; then both runners moved up on a wild pitch charged to Twins reliever Joe Grzenda. Another intentional walk to Bob Oliver loaded the bases, and Royals manager Joe Gordon sent Joe Keough to the plate as a pinch-hitter for Ellie Rodriguez.

Keough singled to right field off Twins reliever Dick Woodson to score Joe Foy and the Royals had a 4–3 walkoff win. Veteran reliever Moe Drabowsky, the oldest player on the team at 33 (born July 21, 1935), collected the first win as he had retired Roseboro, Charlie Manuel, and Uhlaender 1-2-3 in the top of the 12th inning.

There were many firsts in the game. It was the first game for American League umpire Don Denkinger, who manned third base to begin his 20-year career. Sixteen years later, Royals history and Denkinger would cross paths again for a memorable moment in the 1985 World Series. It was also the first major-league managerial game for Billy Martin, who would lead the 1969 Twins to the first American League Western Division title. Most important, it was a perfect trifecta for the Royals—their first game, first win, and first walkoff win, all in three hours and 17 minutes.

Did You Know?—*The Minnesota Twins are the relocated Washington Senators, who were part of the American League for its first season as a major league in 1901. Those same Washington Senators were the relocated Kansas City Blues from the 1900 American League in its last season as a minor league.*

8. Amos Otis, John Mayberry, Cookie Rojas, and Billy Butler.

The 1973 Major League Baseball All-Star Game was played on July 24, 1973 at brand-new Royals Stadium. For

Kansas City, it was great to host the Midsummer Classic for the first time since the Athletics hosted the first of two All-Star Games played in 1960. For the Royals, it was great because it marked the first time a member of the Royals was in the American League starting lineup.

Royals center fielder Amos Otis was already a three-time All-Star, having been named as a reserve in each of the three previous years—1970, 1971, and 1972. This time it made four consecutive All-Star selections for Otis, and more than that, he became the first Royals player ever voted into the American League starting lineup by baseball fans. Even better, the start would come in his home ballpark.

But Otis wasn't the only Royals player to take the field at the start of the game. First baseman John Mayberry received his first All-Star selection as an American League reserve. However, the elected starter at first base, Dick Allen of the Chicago White Sox, was injured. Oakland manager Dick Williams was managing the American League squad, and he made Mayberry the starter in place of Allen.

Royals second baseman Cookie Rojas was also chosen as an American League reserve—which was his third consecutive selection as a member of the Royals (1971 and 1972). All three players would play in the game. Otis was 2-for-2 with an RBI single in the bottom of the second, scoring Reggie Jackson with the first run of the game. He added a leadoff single in the bottom of the fourth. Mayberry was 1-for-2 with a third-inning walk, and a leadoff double in the bottom of the sixth. Rojas replaced Rod Carew in the top of the sixth and took an eight-inning walk in his only at-bat.

The 2012 Major League All-Star Game was played on July 10 at a newly renovated Kauffman Stadium. This time the Royals only had one representative on the American League team. Designated hitter Billy Butler was chosen as a reserve behind starter David Ortiz of the Red Sox.

Texas manager Ron Washington, a Royals Baseball Academy graduate, was managing the American League squad and sent Butler to the plate as a pinch-hitter for Ortiz leading off the bottom of the seventh inning. Facing the Phillies' Cole Hamels, Butler grounded out to Mets third baseman David Wright.

9. Six.

All of Royals history has been played during the era of the 162-game regular season, so playing every game would mean 162 games played—except for the fact there have been times when games were lost and not made up. So Paul Schaal, the first player to play every game in a single regular season for the Royals, played 161 contests.

Schaal started at third base in every game the Royals played in 1971. Schaal played all or parts of six seasons for the Royals from 1969 through 1974. His 1971 season was one of his best, hitting .274 with career highs in both home runs with 11 and RBIs with 63.

The second Royals single-season iron-man was outfielder Al Cowens in his outstanding 1977 campaign. Cowens made 152 starts that season—125 in right field, 26 in center field, and one at DH. He also played in the other 10 games, primarily as a late-inning defensive replacement, making it into all 162 games. He had his triple crown of career bests, hitting .312 with 23 home runs and 112 RBIs.

That same season, Hal McRae played in all 162 regular-season games. Settling into the designated hitter role, McRae made 113 starts as the Royals DH—but also made 44 starts in left field. He appeared in five other games as a pinch-hitter or defensive replacement. McRae hit .298 with 21 home runs and 92 RBIs—the home run and RBI totals only topped by his career-best totals of 27 and 133 in 1982.

Johnny Damon was the fourth Royals player to appear in every game of a regular season in 1998. Damon played all around the outfield, making 127 starts in center field, 22 starts in right field, and two starts in left field. He played in the 10 other games primarily as a defensive replacement. His power also started to appear, going from eight home runs in 1997 to 18 in 1998, starting a string of 11 of 12 seasons he would hit double-digit big-league home runs.

In 2014, Alcides Escobar became the first Royals shortstop to start all 162 games of a single season. He played all but 16 innings during the 2014 regular season—then started all 15 of the 2014 American League Champion Royals' postseason games as well.

Carlos Beltran played all 162 games of the 2002 regular season. Beltran made 149 starts in center field and 12 starts as the Royals DH. He made one pinch-hit appearance on August 20 that year and grounded out while hitting for third baseman Kit Pellow in the top of the eighth inning of a Royals 6–5 win in 12 innings at Toronto. Beltran hit .273 with 105 RBIs, and his Royals career-best season with 29 home runs.

The sixth Royals player to play every regular-season game did so in the Royals' 2014 American League Championship year of 2014 (a feat that he repeated again in 2016). Alcides Escobar started all 162 of the Royals regular season games at shortstop in 2014. In fact, Escobar was in the field at shortstop for all but 16 innings. He joined Paul Schaal as the only two players in Royals history to start every game of a single regular season—and they both made every start at only one position (third base for Schaal, shortstop for Escobar).

10. Hal and Brian McRae; John and Dusty Wathan; Floyd and Brian Bannister

The simple act of a parent and child playing catch is one of the experiences that makes baseball special and nearly universal. One lament of major-league dads is time missed at home—they often don't see the joy of a child's daily pursuits, whether they are on a field of play or elsewhere. But Hal McRae, John Wathan, and Floyd Bannister got to see something more—each of those Royals saw their son's big-league dreams come true—also in a Royals uniform.

The McRaes, Hal and Brian, made major-league history in Royals uniforms, becoming the first father and son to play together on the same major-league team during spring training in 1986—four years before the Griffeys, Ken and Ken Junior,

Hal and Brian McRae became the first major-league father and son to play together during a spring training game on March 13, 1986. Hal later became only the fourth father to manage his son in the major leagues when he skippered the Royals from 1991 to 1994.

did the same during the regular season with Seattle. Hal was finishing his Royals Hall of Fame career, entering his penultimate season as a player, while Brian was the club's 1985 first-round draft pick in his first spring camp as a player. In 1991, Hal would return to the Royals as manager with Brian as the Royals' starting center fielder. Hal had the added bonus of becoming one of the few fathers to ever manage his son in the big leagues.

The Wathans are the epitome of a baseball family. John played his entire big-league career with the Royals and later managed the club. All those seasons in Kansas City meant his children grew up at Royals Stadium and oldest son Dusty made it to the big leagues just like his dad. Dusty played 14 seasons in the minors before he finally got his big-league opportunity with the 2002 Royals. Also like his dad, Dusty stayed in baseball after his playing career and became a minor-league manager.

The Bannisters were mirror images on the mound; Floyd threw from the left side, and Brian from the right. Floyd was the first overall pick in the 1976 draft by the Astros and reached the big leagues the next year. He was traded from the White Sox to Kansas City for the 1988 season. Brian followed in his dad's footsteps, coming to the Royals in a trade with the Mets in 2006. Though they had very different styles, both father and son posted seasons with double-figure wins for the Royals.

11. Steve Busby (twice), Jim Colborn, and Bret Saberhagen.

In 1971 Kansas City drafted Steve Busby and a memorable career began. He led the University of Southern California to the 1971 College World Series Championship before his major-league debut in 1972. The next year he was the Royals' Opening Day starter in his rookie season. In just his 10th major-league start, Busby threw the first no-hitter in Royals history on April 27, 1973.

It wasn't the smoothest or easiest no-hitter in history, as Busby walked six Tigers and only recorded four strikeouts. The Royals got all the offense they needed when Ed Kirkpatrick led off the top of the fifth inning with a home run off Tigers starter Jim Perry. Amos Otis later added another solo home run in the top of the eighth.

In the bottom of the ninth inning, Busby walked leadoff man Duke Sims, but was saved when Rich Reese lined out to first baseman John Mayberry who doubled off Sims. The final out was a groundout to shortstop Fred Patek by Tigers catcher Bill Freehan. The Royals won the game 3–0 at Tiger Stadium in Detroit—it was the first no-hitter thrown at Tiger Stadium since Virgil Trucks threw the first of his two 1952 season no-hitters on May 15, 1952.

The Busby no-hitter was the first of four in the American League in 1973 (two of those by Nolan Ryan); Phil Niekro also threw a no-hitter for the Braves in the National League that season. In the first year of the designated hitter rule in the American League, the Busby no-hitter was the first in Major League Baseball history in which the opposing pitcher did not bat.

Busby was at it again the following season, when he threw a second no-hitter on June 19, 1974 against the Brewers at County Stadium in Milwaukee. The Royals took a 1–0 lead in the top of the second after a leadoff walk to John Mayberry, a two-out walk to Al Cowens, and an RBI single from rookie third baseman George Brett.

Cookie Rojas played a key role in the no-hit bid with the defensive play of the game. With two outs in the bottom of the eighth, Brewers rookie Bob Hansen hit a hard groundball that looked like it was headed to right field—before the second baseman quickly moved to his left and cut it off with a diving stop and threw to first to retire the side.

In the ninth, Busby struck out Bob Coluccio looking, retired Tim Johnson on a fly ball to center field, and ended the no-hit effort by getting Don Money to pop out to Rojas. Busby was nearly perfect. His only mistake was a second-inning lead-off walk to George Scott—after Busby had been ahead in the count 0-2. The Royals defeated the Brewers 2–0.

Jim Colborn was the second Royals pitcher to toss a no-hitter when he blanked the Rangers on May 14, 1977 at Royals Stadium. Colborn's was probably the least likely of the Royals' no-hitters, but it counted just the same.

The Royals had three RBI triples in the game, but only the first one was necessary. Dave Nelson walked with two outs in the bottom of the third and scored the only run the Royals needed when Tom Poquette followed with an RBI triple to put the Royals ahead 1–0.

Jim Colborn was a most unlikely no-hit pitcher when he took the mound for Kansas City that day. He hit a batter in the fifth and walked another in the sixth, then relied on the defensive skills of his teammates, including a couple of gems by outfielder Tom Poquette.

Colborn retired the first 14 Rangers in order before Toby Harrah reached on a hit-by-pitch with two outs in the top of the fifth inning. The only other Rangers baserunner was future Royals catcher Jim Sundberg, who coaxed a leadoff walk in the top of the sixth inning. Sundberg was immediately eliminated on a 6-4-3 double play off the bat of Juan Beniquez (another future Royals player).

Colborn retired the final 11 Rangers batters in order, the last being Claudell Washington on a groundball to first baseman Pete LaCock. Colborn was the first Royals pitcher to toss a no-hitter at home as the Royals defeated Texas 6–0. It was the 199th no-hitter in Major League Baseball history.

In his eighth season with the Royals, it seemed the only thing Bret Saberhagen had not accomplished was throwing a no-hitter. He changed that on August 26, 1991 at Royals Stadium against the Chicago White Sox.

The Royals scored all the runs Saberhagen needed in the bottom of the first inning. Brian McRae led off with a single; Kirk Gibson walked; then McRae went to third on a passed ball by White Sox starter Charlie Hough and scored on a sacrifice fly by George Brett.

Bret Saberhagen celebrates after his no-hitter against the Chicago White Sox on August 26, 1991 at Royals Stadium. Saberhagen was the third pitcher to toss a no-hitter in Royals franchise history.

The White Sox only recorded three baserunners in the game. The first was a Saberhagen walk to catcher Ron Karkovice with one out in the top of the third inning. The key play of the game came with one out in the top of the fifth when Dan Pasqua's fly ball to left glanced off the glove of left fielder Kirk Gibson. The scoreboard at Royals Stadium briefly displayed a "1" in the hit column, but official scorer Del Black had not yet made his call. After watching a couple of replay angles, he ruled the play an error on Gibson.

From there, Saberhagen retired 14 of the last 15 batters he faced—walking Pasqua leading off the top of the eighth. The final out was a hard groundball to second baseman Terry Shumpert off the bat of future Hall of Famer Frank Thomas. The Royals defeated the White Sox 7–0 in what would be the second-to-last home win of Saberhagen's Royals Hall of Fame career.

Did You Know?—*The first of National Baseball Hall of Fame pitcher Nolan Ryan's major-league–record seven career no-hitters was thrown on May 15, 1973 against the Royals at Royals Stadium.*

12. Jim Eisenreich.

Jim Eisenreich was born in St. Cloud, Minnesota. He attended Technical High School and played baseball for the Tech Tigers in St. Cloud. He attended St. Cloud State University and played baseball for the St. Cloud State Huskies.

Eisenreich was selected in the 16th round of the 1980 June draft by the Minnesota Twins. He made his major-league debut batting leadoff for the Twins on Opening Day April 6, 1982 at the Hubert H. Humphrey Metrodome in Minneapolis, Minnesota. It was the first game for the Twins in their new home ballpark, and they lost 11–7 to the Mariners.

Minnesota and Jim Eisenreich go together. But the perfect hometown-boy-makes-good story was interrupted not long after it started. The 23-year-old Eisenreich played 34 games

with the Twins in 1982, then two more in 1983, then a scant
12 more in 1984. Eisenreich was having trouble breathing on

Outfielder Jim Eisenreich started his career with his home state
Minnesota Twins before playing for the Royals from 1987 to 1992.
He won the Royals' Les Milgram Player of the Year Award in 1989.

the field and struggled to control some body tics. Something was wrong, but nobody knew what it was—least of all Jim. For his best interests—and, he believed, those of the Twins—Eisenreich decided to leave professional baseball.

But he didn't give up the dream of seeing how good he could be in the big leagues. In 1985 and 1986, Eisenreich went home and played amateur baseball again with the St. Cloud Beaudreau's Saints while trying to find out what was ailing him. He finally got the diagnosis of Tourette's Syndrome. With the problem identified, he wanted to know if Tourette's could be managed. When the answer was yes, it made all the difference.

Eisenreich wanted a second chance in professional baseball. The Twins placed him on waivers, thinking that perhaps trying to start there again would be too difficult. The Kansas City Royals placed a waiver claim on Eisenreich and acquired him from Minnesota for the grand total of one dollar on October 10, 1986.

He started the 1987 season with the Royals' Double-A affiliate, the Memphis Chicks of the Southern League. Eisenreich hit .382 with 36 doubles, 10 triples, 11 home runs, 60 runs scored, and 57 RBIs in 70 games with the Chicks. He returned to the big leagues and made his Royals debut on June 22, 1987.

Eisenreich hit .238 in 44 games for the Royals in 1987, then hit only .218 in 82 games with the Royals in 1988. But in 1989, everything seemed to revert back to the storybook beginning of his career. During the season, Eisenreich played 134 games, hitting .293 with nine home runs with a career-best 59 RBIs. He also recorded career bests with 64 runs scored and 27 stolen bases. More importantly he had indeed reignited a big-league career that had seemed stalled, if not over.

The waiver claim of Jim Eisenreich was without question the best one-dollar-investment the Royals organization ever made. Eisenreich played six seasons with the Royals and won the 1989 Royals Player of the Year Award. The second chance for the kid from St. Cloud lasted 13 major-league seasons and he still lives in Kansas City today—so we still have a claim on him (although we proudly share him with his home state of Minnesota).

13. Johnny Damon.

Mention a consecutive-games-played streak in baseball and there are usually two names that come quickly to mind—Lou Gehrig and Cal Ripken. It's also interesting to note that both of those Hall of Famers and their games-played streaks have a tie to Kansas City. More on that in a minute.

But in Royals history the name to know for consecutive games played is Johnny Damon. On September 25, 1997, Damon led off the top of the sixth inning with a single and scored on an RBI double by Jeff King to tie the Brewers 1–1 in a game the Royals went on to win 2–1 at County Stadium in Milwaukee. It was the final game of the season for the Royals center fielder, as he was out of the lineup for the final three games in Chicago.

Damon was back in the lineup for Opening Day in 1998 in Baltimore. Although he went 0-for-4 in that Royals 4–1 win over the Orioles at Camden Yards, Damon started what would become the Royals club record for consecutive games played. Just for fun, Ripken was 0-for-3 in that game, which was #2,479 in his major-league record 2,632 consecutive games played streak.

The Royals mark isn't nearly as long. Damon played every game from March 31, 1998 through the first game of a double-header on September 14, 1999—a streak of 305 consecutive games. He bested the record previously held by Hal McRae, who played 263 consecutive games for the Royals from October 3, 1976 through July 29, 1978.

As for Ripken's ties to Kansas City, the future Hall of Famer made his major-league debut on August 10, 1981 against the Royals at Memorial Stadium in Baltimore. He broke Gehrig's mark playing in his 2,131st consecutive game on September 6, 1995. The next season on June 14, 1996 at Kauffman Stadium, Ripken passed Japan's Sachio Kinugasa for the longest streak in world baseball history at 2,216.

As for Gehrig, his streak ended at 2,130 games when he voluntarily took himself out of the Yankees' starting lineup on May 2, 1939 in Detroit. Gehrig never played another major-league game, but he did play one last game about six weeks later.

The Kansas City Blues were one of New York's top affiliates, and they held Yankee Day at Ruppert Stadium (then the name of the ballpark at 22nd and Brooklyn) on June 12, 1939—an exhibition between the reigning World Series and American Association Champions. The Kansas City crowd of 23,864 clearly wanted to see Gehrig, and he obliged, taking the field for the first three innings. He made four putouts at first base and grounded out in his lone at-bat.

The 2,130 consecutive games are a well-known part of the Gehrig story. What isn't well known is that the "Iron Horse" actually played one last game and it happened in Kansas City.

14. Danny Tartabull.

Danny Tartabull wasn't the first Royals player to post a three home run game, but he was the first to have the longball hat trick at home. It happened during his All-Star season of 1991 when Tartabull hit .316 with 31 home runs and exactly 100 RBIs.

The Royals cleanup hitter got things started with a leadoff homer in the Royals' three-run bottom of the second inning. Unfortunately, Oakland erupted for seven runs in the top of the fourth to take a commanding 8–3 lead. But that didn't stop Tartabull from trying to mount a comeback.

His second home run came with the bases empty and one out in the bottom of the sixth. In the bottom of the eighth, George Brett led off with a double—then Tartabull launched a two-run shot for his third home run of the game. The blast pulled the Royals to within two runs at 9–7.

In the bottom of the ninth, Warren Cromartie had a one-out pinch-hit single to get the tying run to the plate. Brian McRae flew out to center for the second out. Then George Brett lined out to center field to end the game—with a crestfallen Tartabull in the on-deck circle.

Through the 2016 season, the Tartabull performance remains the only three home run game by a Royals player at home in franchise history, and it wasn't enough to win. Be careful what you wish for. . . .

15. 44.

The 1977 Royals are the answer to many "how many" questions in franchise history. One of those is how many games is the most the Royals have ever been over the .500 mark, and the answer is 44 games over .500 on September 25, 1977.

The mark was set with a doubleheader sweep of the Angels in Anaheim—the Royals' fourth consecutive doubleheader sweep in the month of September 1977 (perhaps out of exhaustion, they would be swept in a doubleheader at Oakland on September 27, 1977—their fifth double dip in the month).

In the first game, Royals starter Paul Splittorff outdueled Angels starter Ken Brett. Splittorff tossed six innings, allowing one run on three hits; Brett went 7 ⅔ innings allowing six runs on nine hits (although he did hold his little brother hitless in two at-bats before George left the game).

The Royals were powered by home runs from Fred Patek, tying the game 1–1 with one out in the top of the third inning, and Hal McRae, who put the Royals in front with a leadoff home run in the fourth. The Royals went on to coast to a 6–3 win.

In the second game, Al Cowens broke a 2–2 tie with a two-run triple off Nolan Ryan that started the scoring in the Royals' four-run top of the seventh inning. Marty Pattin threw a complete game, scattering eight hits with no walks and six strikeouts, and the Royals completed the sweep with a 6–2 victory.

The two wins were the Royals' 10th and 11th consecutive road victories to set a then club record and the sweep boosted their record to 99-55—the 44 games over .500 was the high water mark in club history for any single season. The sweep also completed an eight-game winning streak—and concluded a stretch in which the Royals won 24 of 25 games, and an amazing 35 of their last 39.

16. Bud Blattner.

The Kansas City Royals were brand new in 1969, but their lead broadcaster was a seasoned veteran. The first Voice of the Royals was Robert Garnett Blattner—better known as "Bud" or "Buddy" Blattner. The broadcast booth was familiar territory for Blattner, and the Royals were in good hands, and of course good voice as well.

Blattner was an athlete turned broadcaster, although he made his lasting mark in the booth. Before turning to baseball, Blattner had been a world-class table tennis player as a teenager. He won the 1936 World's Men's Doubles Championship with teammate Jimmy McClure in Prague. Blattner holds a place in the USA Table Tennis Hall of Fame.

Blattner, who was born and raised in St. Louis, signed with the St. Louis Cardinals in 1938 and worked his way to the big leagues. He made his major-league debut with the Cardinals on April 18, 1942. He played 19 games that season before being claimed on waivers by the New York Giants. By that time Blattner had also been drafted by the US Navy. He served in the Pacific Theater during World War II, primarily stationed on the island of Guam.

After the war Blattner returned to baseball, playing three seasons with the New York Giants from 1946 to 1948. He played one final season with the Philadelphia Phillies in 1949. He later explained that at that point he knew his baseball skills were "shot" as he put it, but his love for the game was still strong. Blattner decided that broadcasting might be his best path to staying in the game.

His broadcast career started back home in St. Louis when he was paired with Dizzy Dean in 1950 as the broadcast team for the American League St. Louis Browns. The pairing of the smooth-toned steadiness of Blattner and the homespun antics of Dean was a hit. The two also called games nationally, including a stint as the television tandem for the Game of the Week on NBC and CBS.

Blattner moved crosstown to work with the Cardinals for two years in 1960 and 1961, then went west to become the lead voice for the expansion Los Angeles Angels, then in their second year. He remained with the Angels through 1968 when a chance to get closer to home opened with the expansion Kansas City Royals.

Blattner was at the mic for the first pitch in Royals history on April 8, 1969 from Wally Bunker and the first hit by Lou Piniella. But it was his junior partner that called the Joe Keough RBI single that made the Royals walkoff winners in 12 innings.

Blattner was hired as the lead broadcaster for the Royals and was given full power to choose his partner. After listening to many audition tapes, Blattner decided on 25-year-old Dennis G. Matthews from Bloomington, Illinois. The Royals' first game was also the first big-league broadcast for Matthews.

Bud Blattner and Denny Matthews were the first radio play-by-play team in Royals history. Blattner was the lead "Voice of the Royals" from 1969 to 1975.

Blattner remained with the club through 1975. But his legacy with the ballclub lasted many decades, as it was Blattner that brought Denny Matthews to Kansas City to begin one of the longest broadcast careers with a single team in Major League Baseball history.

17. 18.

The longest game by number of innings played in Royals history is 18—and it's happened twice.

The first 18-inning marathon for the Royals was at home at Municipal Stadium against the Texas Rangers on May 17, 1972. It was a game of great frustration for the Royals on many accounts, starting with a three-run top of the first for the Rangers against starter Dick Drago.

The Royals chipped away with an RBI double from Ed Kirkpatrick in the second, an RBI single from Cookie Rojas in the fourth, and Gail Hopkins got the Royals even with an RBI double in the seventh. The Royals had the bases loaded with no outs in the bottom of the ninth, but a shallow fly ball to center by Fred Patek couldn't score John Mayberry from third. Then another fly ball by Amos Otis followed, and Mayberry tried to make it. He was out at the plate and the game went into extra innings.

In the bottom of the 10th, the Royals got a one-out single from Lou Piniella, a double by Cookie Rojas, and an intentional walk to Dennis Paepke to load the bases for John Mayberry. But Big John hit a hard grounder to second with a drawn-in Rangers infield for a 4-2-3 double play to end the inning. So close, but it was on to the 11th.

In the bottom of the 11th, pitcher Roger Nelson singled with one out and moved to second on a sacrifice bunt by Fred

Patek. The Rangers walked Amos Otis intentionally to face their former teammate Richie Scheinblum. Scheinblum singled to center field and Nelson rounded third with the potential winning run, only to be thrown out at the plate by center fielder Elliott Maddox. More free baseball, lots more.

The Rangers had scored three runs in the top of the first inning; then Royals pitching held them scoreless for 16 consecutive frames—until the 18th. With one out, the Rangers' Joe Lovitto was awarded first base on a catcher's interference call against the Royals' Dennis Paepke. Rangers pitcher Jim Panther laid down a sacrifice bunt attempt, but pitcher Ted Abernathy's throw to first got away.

Then an intentional walk loaded the bases for the Rangers. Toby Harrah followed with a groundball that glanced off the glove of pitcher Tom Murphy. The Royals got the force-out at second, but Lovitto crossed the plate with the go-ahead run. Arrrghhhhh.

The Royals went down 1-2-3 in the bottom of the inning and the Rangers walked away with a 4–3 win in a doubleheader's worth of innings. It would take 19 years for the Royals to extract some revenge, but revenge would be had.

The second 18-inning marathon for the Royals was also at home and it also came against the Texas Rangers—this time at Royals Stadium on Thursday, June 6, 1991. The afternoon game featured a much-ballyhooed pitching matchup that had been talked about for well over a week between Bret Saberhagen and Nolan Ryan, which attracted 38,523 fans.

Both star pitchers did what was expected. Saberhagen held a 2–0 lead before allowing the Rangers to tie the game with a pair of seventh-inning runs. Saberhagen allowed two runs on five hits over seven innings. Ryan also went seven innings, allowing two runs on six hits. Neither would be involved in the decision.

The Rangers briefly took the lead when Mario Diaz scored on a two-out RBI single by Julio Franco. But Carmelo Martinez, pinch-hitting for Warren Cromartie, hit a leadoff home run in the bottom of the ninth to get the Royals back even at 3–3.

The Royals left the bases loaded in the bottom of the 11th. The Rangers left the bases loaded in the top of the 12th. The Royals left the bases loaded in the bottom of the 13th. Both teams left the bases loaded in the 15th inning. There were missed opportunities everywhere.

After 17 innings, the Royals had used everyone in their bullpen and turned to Mike Boddicker, who had started and won the first game of the series two days earlier. He tossed a 1-2-3 top of the 18th inning. The end was (hopefully) near.

In the bottom of the 18th inning, Kevin Seitzer led off with a single and moved to second when Rangers starter-turned-reliever Kenny Rogers walked Brent Mayne. Kurt Stillwell then laid down a sacrifice bunt, and Rogers threw wildly to third, allowing Seitzer to cross home plate with the winning run.

The game lasted 18 innings and went six hours and 28 minutes—both Royals records. And it ended on an error, of course. The Royals had exacted 18 innings of revenge against the Rangers by the same 4–3 score.

Two of my favorite notes from that game: First, catcher Brent Mayne caught every pitch of the game for the Royals—all 354 of them. Second, the game that started around lunchtime and ended well after the dinner hour resulted in quite a few concession sales, reported to include 8,738 hot dogs, 3,077 Polish sausages, 2,818 colossal hot dogs, 448 bratwursts,

840 hamburgers and cheeseburgers, 587 barbecue sandwiches, 1,496 slices of pepperoni pizza, 478 slices of deluxe pizza, 4,424 orders of nachos, 4,169 malts, 1,101 sundaes, 1,922 Snickers bars, 56 Italian sausages, 75 chicken sandwiches, and 63,310 beverage sales.

18. Mike Sweeney.

The Royals' record for consecutive games with a home run is held by Royals Hall of Famer Mike Sweeney. The Royals first baseman connected for home runs in five consecutive games from June 25 through June 29 of the 2002 season.

In the first game of the streak on June 25, 2002, the Tigers scored four runs in the top of the first inning, powered by back-to-back home runs by Robert Fick and Brandon Inge. Mike Sweeney started the Royals' scoring with a leadoff home run in the bottom of the second inning.

Carlos Beltran reached with a one-out single in the bottom of the third. Mike Sweeney followed with a double; then with two outs Raul Ibanez tripled to score them both and put the Royals ahead 5–4. With the score tied 5–5 with two outs in the bottom of the fifth inning, Joe Randa singled and Raul Ibanez followed with a two-run home run to regain the lead for the Royals 7–5. The Royals defeated Detroit 8–6 at Kauffman Stadium.

In the second game of the streak on June 26, 2002, Sweeney again started the Royals' scoring, with a one-out solo home run in the bottom of the fourth to tie the game at 1–1. The two teams traded single runs in both the fifth and sixth. The Tigers got one in the top of the seventh, but the Royals took the lead on a three-run home run by Aaron Guiel in the bottom of the inning. The Royals defeated Detroit 6–4 at Kauffman Stadium.

In the third game of the streak on June 27, 2002, Sweeney plated the Royals' first run for the third consecutive contest, this time with a leadoff home run in the bottom of the second. The lead held and the Royals cruised to a 5–2 win over Detroit at Kauffman Stadium.

In the fourth game of the streak on June 28, 2002, Sweeney posted the fifth five-RBI game of his career, and the Royals needed them all and more after the Padres scored five runs in the top of the first. His first RBI in the contest came on a two-run home run in the bottom of the third that narrowed the Royals' deficit to 6–3.

Sweeney later capped the Royals' go-ahead five-run bottom of the seventh inning with a bases-loaded double, scoring three runs to give the Royals a 13–9 lead. The Royals would get their first-ever win over San Diego 14–10 at Kauffman Stadium.

In game five of the streak on June 29, 2002, Sweeney launched a two-run home run with one out in the bottom of the sixth to give the Royals a brief 3–1 lead. The Padres regained the lead with three runs in the top of the seventh.

Michael Tucker led off the bottom of the seventh with a home run to get the Royals back to even, but Ron Gant's grand slam in the top of the 10th inning was too much to overcome. The Royals lost to the San Diego Padres 8–4 at Kauffman Stadium.

Over the five-game stretch Sweeney hit a robust, and numerically appropriate, .555 (10-for-18) with four doubles, five home runs, and 10 RBIs.

19. One.

Mike Sweeney had 215 homers in his big-league career—197 of those with the Royals and only one against Kansas City. He was so very close to two career home run milestones: three from being the second Royals player to reach 200, and one away from an even 100 hit at Kauffman Stadium as a Royal (he did hit one at Kauffman Stadium as a Mariner).

Sweeney's last home run with the Royals came on June 8, 2007 against the Phillies at Kauffman Stadium. Reigning National League Most Valuable Player Ryan Howard had put the Phillies in front with a two-run home run in the top of the first inning. Greg Dobbs made it 3–0 Phillies with a solo shot in the top of the second.

The Royals rallied with six runs in the bottom of the second. Mark Grudzielanek hit a two-run home run that put the Royals in front 4–3. Then after a walk to Mark Teahen, Mike Sweeney launched another two-run home run to make it 6–4 Royals. It was the first time the Royals had hosted the Phillies in Kansas City since the pivotal Game 5 of the 1980 World Series won by Philadelphia 4–3 at Royals Stadium on October 19, 1980. This time the Royals won 8–4 at Kauffman Stadium.

The lone home run Sweeney hit against the Royals came a little more than two years later when he returned as a member of the Seattle Mariners on August 6, 2009 at Kauffman Stadium.

Against future Royals pitcher Jason Vargas, the Royals opened that game with five runs on five hits in the bottom of the first inning, highlighted by a Billy Butler two-run home run. The Mariners scored their first run with one out in the top of the fourth inning, when Mike Sweeney launched a solo home run off Royals starter Bruce Chen.

The Royals would win 8–2 and Bruce Chen picked up the first of 47 career wins with the Royals. But Sweeney finally got that 100th career home run at Kauffman Stadium—the one and only of his 215 career home runs to come against the Royals.

20. Blake Stein.

In one of the most forgettable starts to ever match an impressive American League pitching record, Blake Stein earned his way into the history book by striking out eight consecutive Brewers on June 17, 2001 at Miller Park in Milwaukee. He gave up five hits and four runs over 5 ⅔ innings, but mixed in 11 strikeouts among 17 outs he recorded—including eight in succession.

Stein began his streak with two outs in the first when he struck out Richie Sexson swinging to end the inning. He then struck out Devon White, Ronnie Belliard, and Luis Lopez in the second. Then he struck out the side again in the third, ringing up Henry Blanco, Jamey Wright, and Alex Sanchez. He finished his run by catching Mark Loretta looking to start the bottom of the fourth. The eight strikeouts in a row tied a then American League record accomplished before by only three pitchers—Nolan Ryan (twice), Ron Davis, and Roger Clemens.

Two batters later, he surrendered a home run to Richie Sexson that tied the game 1–1. The Brewers scored three more in the bottom of the sixth, and Royals manager Tony Muser lifted Stein after he had thrown 92 pitches. On the plus side, Stein had a career-best 11 strikeouts. On the negative side, he and the Royals took a 5–2 loss to the Brewers.

On the really negative side, Doug Fister of the Tigers bested Stein, Ryan, Davis, and Clemens by striking out nine consecutive batters on September 27, 2012 at Comerica Park in Detroit—and set the record against the Royals. The Royals didn't go without a fight that Thursday afternoon, as the Tigers needed a run in the bottom of the ninth to defeat the Royals 5–4.

21. Tony Pena.

The Royals had the best record of all the 1969 expansion teams. The Royals had posted a winning record in only the third year of the franchise. The Royals had won multiple division titles, two American League pennants, and a World Series title. The Royals had collected an American League MVP, three Cy Young Awards, and three Rookie of the Year Awards. Yet until 2003, no Royals skipper had ever won American League Manager of the Year honors.

The 2003 Royals started with a nine-game winning streak—the best start in franchise history and the first team to have such a start since Cincinnati in 1990. It was only the 14th such start in the history of Major League Baseball: all the more impressive, and perhaps improbable, as the Royals were rebounding from the first-ever franchise season with 100 losses in 2002.

The 2003 Royals finished the season with a winning record at 83-79. It was the first winning season for the Royals since they ended the strike-shortened 1994 season at 64-51, and their first full-season winning campaign since closing out 1993 at 84-78. The 83 wins were the sixth best turnaround in baseball history for a club that lost 100 games the prior year.

After the season, Pena was named the 2003 American League Manager of the Year by the Baseball Writers Association of America. He won 24 of the 28 first-place votes to far outdistance the Twins' Ron Gardenhire, who managed Minnesota to the 2003 American League Central Division title.

Interesting to note, at 44 years old Pena was one of the youngest managers to win the honor. The 2003 National League Manager of the Year was Jack McKeon, who at 72 years old was the oldest manager to ever win the award—the same

Jack McKeon who managed his first major-league game at age 43 with the 1973 Kansas City Royals.

Did You Know?—*National Baseball Hall of Famer and Royals Hall of Fame manager Whitey Herzog is the only person to wear the uniforms of the Kansas City Blues, Kansas City Athletics, and Kansas City Royals in an on-field role. Whitey played for the 1952 Kansas City Blues; he played for the Kansas City Athletics from 1958 to 1960; and he managed the Royals from 1975 to 1979.*

22. Bob Schaefer.

This is close to being a "look quick or you might have missed it" question and answer in Royals history. From Joe Gordon through Ned Yost, there have been 16 full-time managers in Royals history. But four times in the transition from one manager to the next the Royals were led by an interim skipper, and on two of those occasions they turned to Bob Schaefer.

Mike Ferraro was the first interim manager in Royals history. Ferraro was serving as the Royals third base coach when he took the reins after the 1986 All-Star break when Dick Howser was first diagnosed with the brain cancer that took his life the following year. Ferraro led the Royals through the very rough waters of the second half of the 1986 season, finishing with a 36-38 record.

Bob Schaefer first joined the Royals organization in 1987 when he became manager of the Memphis Chicks, the Royals' Double-A affiliate in the Southern League. He moved to the big-league club in 1988 as first base coach during the first full year John Wathan was manager of the Royals. He served in that role through the 1990 season, then became Wathan's bench coach in 1991.

When Wathan was relieved of his duties following the Royals game on May 21, 1991, and before Hal McRae was hired and managed his first game on May 23, 1991, the Royals turned to Schaefer as their interim manager. He only managed a single game, but what a crazy game it turned out to be.

The long and short of it was the pitching matchup, featuring 6'10" Randy Johnson for the Mariners against 5'9" Tom Gordon for the Royals. Seattle's Greg Briley and Harold Reynolds started the game with back-to-back singles off Tom Gordon. The Mariners did not score in the inning and would only get two more hits the rest of the game.

In the bottom of the first, Kirk Gibson led off with a walk and with one out Brian McRae coaxed another. With runners on first and second Danny Tartabull popped an infield fly, which was dropped by Seattle third baseman Edgar Martinez. However, Brian McRae took off from first and passed Kirk Gibson at second base, resulting in a double play to end the inning.

The Royals did score in the fifth inning after one-out singles by Jim Eisenreich and Carmelo Martinez and a two-out walk to Kirk Gibson loaded the bases. Eisenreich scored the first run of the game on a Randy Johnson wild pitch. The Royals scored two more in the seventh after walks to Carmelo Martinez and Kirk Gibson. Martinez scored on an RBI single from Kurt Stillwell—Gibson on an RBI single by Brian McRae.

Johnson only allowed four singles, but walked eight over 6 ⅓ innings. Tom Gordon threw a four-hit complete game, but lost the shutout on a Ken Griffey solo homer with two outs in the ninth. The Royals defeated Seattle 3–1 at Royals Stadium and Bob Schaefer had a perfect 1-0 career mark as a major-league manager.

Schaefer returned to the field with the Royals when he was named to the staff of manager Tony Pena in 2002. He was right back in the role of bench coach with Pena throughout his Royals tenure. Then when Pena resigned on May 10, 2005, the Royals again turned to Schaefer as interim manager.

Schaefer's second stint as interim Royals manager was a little longer, encompassing 17 games through the hiring of Buddy Bell on May 30, 2005. He lost his perfect record in the first game when the Royals could not hold a 9–7 lead, allowing the Blue Jays to score five runs in the bottom of the eighth inning in a 12–9 loss at SkyDome in Toronto.

The Royals were 5-12 in Schaefer's second interim stay as manager—including six consecutive losses to close out the stretch. But they did rebound to sweep the New York Yankees at Kauffman Stadium in Buddy Bell's first three games as Royals manager.

23. Fred Patek.

The first player to hit for the cycle in Royals history was Royals Hall of Famer Fred Patek on July 9, 1971 against the Twins at Metropolitan Stadium in Bloomington, Minnesota. And as the Royals leadoff hitter, he got things going from the very first at-bat.

Patek started the game with a double against Twins starter Jim Perry. He then scored the first run when Paul Schaal followed with an RBI single. In the top of the second, Bobby Knoop started a Royals rally with a one-out single; with two outs Patek singled and Paul Schaal walked to load the bases. Amos Otis followed with a two-RBI single and the Royals led 3–0.

The Twins scored three runs in the bottom of the third inning to tie the game. With two outs in the top of the fourth,

Patek tripled, but was left stranded. With the game still tied 3–3 in the top of the ninth, Knoop again started a Royals rally with another one-out single. With two outs, Fred Patek launched a two-run home run to give the Royals the lead and complete the first cycle in club history.

It was only the second home run in Patek's Royals career, but was perfectly timed for both the Royals and their new shortstop. Paul Schaal made it back-to-back home runs when he followed with another just for good measure, and the Royals defeated the Twins 6–3.

24. George Brett and Frank White.

George Brett and Frank White were the dynamic duo in the first championship era of Royals history. They played on some great Royals teams with many great teammates. They were both outstanding on their own. Royals fans had the privilege of watching them together for many years. So perhaps it should not be surprising that hitting for the cycle—twice—is another in the long list of accomplishments the two share in Royals history.

The first for George came on May 28, 1979 against the Orioles at Royals Stadium. It was one for the ages, and you aged yourself if you saw it because it came in a 16-inning game that wouldn't end.

Willie Wilson led off the bottom of the third inning with a single and scored on a one-out triple by George Brett to tie the game 1–1. Brett would put the Royals in front when he scored on a sacrifice fly by Darrell Porter. With the Royals trailing 3–2 in the bottom of the eighth inning, Steve Braun singled with one out and Brett followed with a two-run home run to put the Royals back ahead 4–3. But Baltimore's Ken

Singleton tied the game with a leadoff home run in the top of the ninth inning.

In extra innings, George singled with one out in the bottom of the 10th inning—but was wiped out in a double play. He was walked intentionally in the bottom of the 12th inning, but was left stranded. He actually completed the cycle with a one-out double in the bottom of the 14th inning. But again, he was left stranded and the game continued.

With the cycle already in hand, and with the game two minutes from entering its fifth hour, George Brett led off the bottom of the 16th inning with a walkoff home run. He was the last player in the 20th century to have two homers in a game in which he hit for the cycle. Brett almost hit for the cycle in extra innings alone with a single, double, home run, and a walk—he reached base in all four extra-inning plate appearances before finally putting an emphatic end to a 5–4 16-inning win.

Later that same season, Frank White hit for the cycle on September 26, 1979 against the Angels at Anaheim Stadium. Frank got his big game started with a two-out single in the top of the first inning, but he was left stranded. Willie Wilson led off the top of the third with a single and scored when Frank put the Royals in front 2–0 with a two-run home run off Angels starter Dave LaRoche.

Frank doubled with two outs in the top of the fifth inning, but was left stranded. He completed his first cycle with two outs in the top of the ninth inning. White tripled to the wall in center field and scored when center fielder Bobby Clark's throw to third eluded third baseman Jim Anderson. His run completed a 4–0 Royals win as Dennis Leonard tossed a five-hit shutout.

The second cycle for Frank White came on August 3, 1982 against Detroit at Royals Stadium. This time he got the proceedings started with a bang. Willie Wilson led off the bottom of the first inning with a single and Frank followed by tagging Tigers starting pitcher Pat Underwood with a two-run home run.

White doubled with two outs in the bottom of the third, but was left stranded. The Royals trailed 5–4 in the bottom of the seventh inning when Willie Wilson lofted a fly ball to center field that center fielder Glenn Wilson misplayed. Willie Wilson ended up at third base and Frank White immediately cashed in on the error for the Royals, scoring Wilson with an RBI single to tie the game at 5–5.

The game remained tied into the bottom of the ninth, when Onix Concepcion reached with a one-out single. With two outs, Frank White tripled to drive in Concepcion for a walkoff 6–5 Royals win and completed the second cycle of his Royals Hall of Fame career in exhilarating fashion.

The second cycle for George Brett came on July 25, 1990 against the Blue Jays at SkyDome in Toronto. Hitting in the cleanup spot in the order, George had the Royals' third single in the two-run, four-hit top of the first inning against Blue Jays starter Todd Stottlemyre.

George started the Royals two-run rally in the top of the third with a one-out triple. He would score on a groundout RBI from Jim Eisenreich. Brett then led off the top of the fifth inning with a double against former Royals pitcher Frank Wills. He scored his second run of the game on a two-out RBI double by Jeff Schulz, making it 5–0 Royals.

George led off the top of the seventh with a home run to cap the Royals' scoring and complete the second cycle of his career. Going into the game Brett was hitting .296—up from the .267 he was hitting at the All-Star break just a few weeks earlier on July 8. This cycle took him over the .300 mark (.304) for the first time in the 1990 season in which he hit a blazing .388 during the second half en route to his third career batting title. The Royals went on to defeat the Blue Jays 6–1.

Through the 2015 season, only 30 players have hit for the cycle multiple times in their major-league careers. The only two players in Major League Baseball history to hit for the cycle multiple times as teammates are Royals Hall of Famers George Brett and Frank White.

25. The question is a query with a rather high quotient of quandary.

On Sunday, April 13, 1980 the Royals were hosting the Detroit Tigers at Royals Stadium. The game itself was scoreless into the bottom of the fourth inning when Hal McRae hit a leadoff single against the Tigers Dave Rozema. He advanced to second on a groundout by Willie Aikens, then scored on an RBI single by Pete LaCock.

The Royals' starting catcher that day was Jamie Quirk, who went 1-for-4 at the plate with a two-out single in the bottom of the sixth. He was left stranded. Quirk was still behind the plate when Royals starter Paul Splittorff was in a tight jam in the top of the seventh. He allowed a leadoff single to Lance Parrish and with one out walked pinch-hitter Champ Summers.

The Royals needed a double play, and Royals manager Jim Frey went to his bullpen for his sinker specialist, reliever Dan Quisenberry. The future Royals Hall of Famer got right what the skipper ordered when he induced a grounder off the bat of pinch-hitter Richie Hebner that glanced off Quisenberry's glove, but was fielded by shortstop U. L. Washington for an unusual 1-6-3 double play to end the threat.

The Royals scored two more runs on a two-out bases-loaded single by Willie Aikens in the bottom of the seventh to

Royals closer Dan Quisenberry had 238 saves in 10 seasons with the Royals, including the first 40-plus save season in major-league history in 1983 (45). He and Jamie Quirk were Royals teammates for eight seasons (1979–1982; 1985–1988).

lead 3–0. Quisenberry pitched a scoreless eighth, but was lifted after surrendering a one-out single to Lance Parrish and a two-out home run to Champ Summers.

Gary Christenson relieved Quisenberry and allowed a double to Richie Hebner, before ending the game with a fly out to right field by Rick Peters. The Royals escaped with a 3–2 win and Gary Christenson picked up the save—the one and only of his brief career.

But it was the pitcher/catcher combination of Quisenberry and Quirk that made the game one for the record books. According to Baseball Reference, through 2016 there have been 47 big-league players with a surname beginning with the letter Q. The Quisenberry and Quirk tandem on April 13, 1980 was the first-ever all-"Q" battery in Major League Baseball history.

HALL OF FAME LEVEL

1. Which two Royals players worked on crews that helped build Royals Stadium? *Answer on page 147.*

2. Who was the first player inducted into the National Baseball Hall of Fame whose plaque noted his time with the Kansas City Royals? *Answer on page 148.*

3. How many starting pitchers did the 1985 World Champion Royals use in the regular season? *Answer on page 152.*

4. The Royals' first designated hitter, the first Royals designated hitter to get a hit, and the first Royals designated hitter to hit a home run—which Royals player(s) accomplished each milestone? *Answer on page 155.*

5. What member of the 1985 world champion Kansas City Royals was selected by the ballclub in its very first draft class during the 1968 June draft? *Answer on page 158.*

6. Who was the last active player from the 1969 Royals inaugural season to appear with the ballclub? *Answer on page 159.*

7. Who was the last active player from the 1985 world championship team to appear with the Royals? *Answer on page 161.*

8. The Royals have played the final game in four major-league ballparks. Can you name them? *Answer on page 164.*

9. Why does George Brett's Hall of Fame plaque in Cooperstown list him with 1,595 career RBIs when he drove in 1,596 runs? *Answer on page 168.*

10. What would the Royals' three retired numbers of 5, 10, and 20 be if they were instead the first numbers worn by the honorees during their Royals careers? *Answer on page 169.*

11. Who was the first hitter to record a multi–home run game for the Kansas City Royals? *Answer on page 171.*

12. Who was the first switch-hitter to record a base hit from both sides of the plate in the same game for the Royals? *Answer on page 173.*

13. What Royals pitcher once recorded four strikeouts in a single inning? *Answer on page 175.*

14. What pitcher was the first to ever throw an "Immaculate Inning"—striking out the side on just nine pitches—for the Royals? *Answer on page 176.*

15. What two players in club history have hit exactly one home run in a Royals uniform with that lone round-tripper being a grand slam? *Answer on page 180.*

16. Who was the first player to wear a Kansas City Royals uniform who was born in Kansas City, Missouri? *Answer on page 182.*

17. Can you name the players who played college baseball at the University of Kansas, Kansas State University, and the University of Missouri–Columbia that went on to play for the Royals? *Answer on page 184.*

18. Three pitchers have won the Cy Young Award as members of the Royals. How many other former Cy Young

Award winners have pitched for the Royals? *Answer on page 188.*

19. Can you name the two sets of brothers to play for the Royals? *Answer on page 192.*

20. How many postseason walkoff wins have the Royals recorded in club history? *Answer on page 196.*

21. What Royals player once stole second, third, and home consecutively in the same inning? *Answer on page 201.*

22. How many former number one overall NFL draft picks were also drafted by the Kansas City Royals? *Answer on page 202.*

23. What is the latest round of the draft the Royals have ever used to select a player who made his way to the big leagues? *Answer on page 205.*

24. What future Royals player had the final College World Series hit at historic Johnny Rosenblatt Stadium in Omaha, Nebraska? *Answer on page 208.*

25. Did Jackie Robinson ever play for the Kansas City Royals? *Answer on page 210.*

HALL OF FAME LEVEL — ANSWERS

1. Today it is difficult to imagine baseball players, at least at the major-league level, needing an offseason job to make ends meet. But there was a time when baseball was simply a spring and summer job for many—and it wasn't all that long ago. Still, it is a rare story when a player helps build a ballpark before playing in it.

Kansas City native and Royals Hall of Famer Frank White was still in the minors when Royals founder Ewing Kauffman helped him get a job working on the new stadium project. The future eight-time Gold Glove winner's tasks included sealing the floors on the third deck, using a chisel and machine to scrape the concrete off concourse support columns (which still stand), and pouring concrete. In his book, *One Man's Dream: My Town, My Team, My Time*, White said he often looked at the field and dreamed he might play there. He would for 18 seasons.

But Frank wasn't alone. Bob Oliver, a member of the original 1969 Royals, also worked on the stadium during the winter of 1971-72. Oliver recalled, "I worked on the sliding pits around the bases and home plate and I rode a few girders and I poured concrete." Unfortunately, his trade to the Angels in May 1972 forestalled Royals Stadium from becoming his "home" ballpark.

Many people in Kansas City had a hand in building the Truman Sports Complex, including Royals Stadium. Another

This aerial photo shows Royals Stadium under construction. The project suffered several delays including two worker strikes that stalled its original planned opening date of 1972. The ballpark debuted at the start of the 1973 season.

person who worked on the project was actor Chris Cooper. The Kansas City native graduated from Southwest High School in 1969 and worked in construction as a young man before getting his start in Hollywood. Cooper won an Academy Award for Best Supporting Actor in the 2002 film *Adaptation*.

2. The first answer that comes to mind for many fans is George Brett. First thought, but not correct. There's ample reason to think that could have been the case, because in many ways George Brett was and remains the quintessential player in franchise history, but he was not the first player to don a Kansas City Royals uniform and be enshrined in Cooperstown.

If you had toured the National Baseball Hall of Fame on July 25, 1999—the very day George Brett was inducted—you would have encountered the plaques of two players who already had their time as members of the Royals commemorated in the most hallowed place in baseball—although admittedly neither of them were really known for their playing days in Kansas City.

The first inducted National Baseball Hall of Famer to have worn a Kansas City Royals uniform was the great Harmon Killebrew, who was enshrined with the Class of 1984 that also included Luis Aparicio, Don Drysdale, Rick Ferrell, and Pee Wee Reese. Killebrew is a Minnesota Twins legend, but his career actually started in 1954 as an 18-year-old bonus baby with the Washington Senators years before their move to the Land of 10,000 Lakes.

Killebrew brought a quiet demeanor and a powerful bat to the Kansas City Royals for what turned out to be his final big-league season in 1975. The soft-spoken slugger was known for booming tape-measure blasts throughout his career—leading the American League in home runs six times and hitting 40 or more in eight different seasons.

National Baseball Hall of Famer Harmon Killebrew spent the final of his 22 major-league seasons with the Kansas City Royals. He appeared in 106 games and hit the last 14 of his 573 career home runs as a member of the 1975 Royals.

Killebrew finished his career with 573 home runs, at the time trailing only Babe Ruth for most in American League history. The final 14 Killebrew home runs came in a Kansas City Royals uniform, and as fate would have it the last of those was hit against the Twins on September 18, 1975 at Metropolitan Stadium in Minnesota.

Harmon Clayton Killebrew was inducted into the National Baseball Hall of Fame on August 12, 1984, becoming the first player to have worn a Kansas City Royals uniform to achieve the game's highest honor. Right there on his plaque it reads Washington A.L. 1954–1960; Minnesota A.L. 1961–1974; and Kansas City A.L. 1975. Although not the first time "Kansas City" appeared on a National Baseball Hall of Fame plaque, it was the first time the reference was made for a member of the Royals.

The second National Baseball Hall of Fame plaque with a Kansas City Royals reference came seven years later when Gaylord Perry was part of the Cooperstown Class of 1991. Perry slipped in with a group that included Rod Carew, Ferguson Jenkins, Tony Lazzeri, and Bill Veeck. Perry played the first decade of his major-league career with the San Francisco Giants, then moved here, there, and everywhere, playing for seven teams in his final dozen years. His storied and colorful career concluded with a brief stint with the 1983 Kansas City Royals.

Perry was known for his array of mound rituals that distracted batters for more than two decades. Of course, part of his mound antics were designed to help conceal where he stashed the Vaseline he used to throw his notorious spitball—which was illegal according to baseball's rules, but somehow Perry was only ejected for throwing the pitch once (August 23, 1982) and even then the umpire could not readily identify whether Perry had any substance on his uniform or person. During his playing days he always denied he threw the illegal pitch, mostly with a smile and a twinkle in his eye, saying it was simply a hard slider.

The hoopla over the spitball, which Perry noted was always much louder when he was going good and less so when he struggled, often obscured the sheer craftsmanship and success the five-time All-Star and two-time Cy Young Award winner had on the mound. Perry reached nearly every magical pitching milestone with 314 wins, 3,534 strikeouts, five 20-win seasons, and a no-hitter. He was also the first pitcher to capture Cy Young Awards in both leagues—winning in 1972 with the Cleveland Indians and again in 1978 with the San Diego Padres.

Perry signed with the Royals on July 6, 1983 after being released by the Seattle Mariners. Although his time with the Royals was short, he was around to play a humorous cameo role in the immortal Pine Tar Game caper at Yankee Stadium on July 24, 1983. Always a thorn in the side of umpires, Perry was again on that fateful afternoon, trying to hide George Brett's infamous bat—this time to no avail; and in the end the Royals were right anyway. For his mischief, he received only his second career ejection.

The final four victories of Perry's Hall of Fame career came as a member of the Kansas City Royals. His last win was a six-hit shutout against the Texas Rangers (another of his many former teams) in Game 1 of a doubleheader on September 3, 1983 at Arlington Stadium.

Gaylord Jackson Perry was inducted into the National Baseball Hall of Fame on July 21, 1991, becoming the second player to have worn a Kansas City Royals uniform to achieve the game's highest honor. His plaque is like a long travel itinerary—San Francisco N.L. 1962–1971; Cleveland A.L. 1972–1975; Texas A.L. 1975–1977, 1980; San Diego N.L. 1978–1979; New York A.L. 1980; Atlanta N.L. 1981; Seattle A.L. 1982–1983—then ends with Kansas City A.L. 1983.

The other that came very close was Hall of Famer Hoyt Wilhelm, who was inducted into the National Baseball Hall of Fame as a member of the Class of 1985. Wilhelm was selected by the Royals with their 25th pick (49th overall) in the American League Expansion Draft from the Chicago White Sox on October 15, 1968. But Wilhelm never actually pitched for the Royals, as they traded him to the California Angels on December 12, 1968 in exchange for Ed Kirkpatrick and Dennis Paepke—both of them members of the inaugural 1969 Kansas City Royals.

3. Seven.

Only seven starting pitchers took the mound for the Royals during their 1985 world championship season. Starting pitching that provides consistency and reliability is often the key to team success, and there is no more clear example in Royals history than the starting staff of Bud Black, Charlie Leibrandt, Bret Saberhagen, Danny Jackson, and Mark Gubicza.

Those five never missed a scheduled start throughout the 1985 season. Perfect attendance for the starting five—*plus some serious talent to be sure*—and the result was a World Series title. Both Bud Black and Charlie Leibrandt led the way with 33 starts each. Bret Saberhagen and Danny Jackson were right behind them with 32 starts apiece, and Mark Gubicza made 28 starts. Two other pitchers made the other four starts.

Steve Farr had been released by the Cleveland Indians at the end of spring training on March 31, 1985. He signed with the Royals on May 9 and began the season with Triple-A Omaha where he went 10-4 over 16 starts (17 appearances) with a sparkling 2.02 ERA.

The Royals called him up to Kansas City on August 8, 1985 and he made his first appearance that night, starting the second game of a doubleheader. Lou Whitaker led off the top of the first with a triple and scored, and the Tigers scored another run in the third. Farr pitched four innings, allowing two runs on five hits. The Royals got him off the hook with three runs in the bottom of the fourth and went on to defeat the Tigers 6–4 at Royals Stadium with Mark Gubicza getting the win in relief. The Royals got the sweep in the twin-bill as the Royals had won game one 10–3 behind a complete game effort by Bret Saberhagen.

Farr started the first game of another doubleheader on September 6, 1985 against the Brewers at Royals Stadium. The Royals scored two in the first, one in the second, and four in the fourth. This time Farr got the victory as he threw five innings, allowing one run on five hits for his first career win with the Royals. He also seemed to be a good luck charm as the Royals again swept the doubleheader, taking the second game 7–4 behind Mark Gubicza. He made a third start for the Royals on September 17 when he and the Royals lost 7–0 to the Mariners at Royals Stadium.

Mike Jones made the last regular season start for the 1985 world champion Royals. Jones was the Royals' first-round selection (21st overall) in the 1977 June draft out of Sutherland High School in Pittsford, New York. He made a quick ascension through the minor leagues.

Jones was 13-6 with a 3.87 ERA with the Royals Double-A affiliate Jacksonville Suns of the Southern League in 1980.

He got a late-season call directly from Double-A to the big leagues on September 1, 1980. He made his major-league debut in relief, closing out an 8–3 loss in Cleveland. On September 20, 1980 he made his first career start, taking a 9–0 loss against Oakland at Royals Stadium. Still, a promising career beckoned. At the time Jones was the second-youngest starting pitcher in Royals history behind only Mark Littell (both since surpassed by Bret Saberhagen).

The next season Jones was 11-7 with a 2.96 ERA at Triple-A Omaha. He was recalled to Kansas City on August 6, 1981 and proceeded to go 6-3 with a 3.21 ERA over 12 major league starts—and he was only 21 years old. Then came the night of December 21, 1981 when Jones was involved in a single-car accident that left him with two dislocated vertebrae. Coming out of the situation, he was lucky to be alive—baseball was suddenly secondary.

He would never quite be the same, but he did make a comeback. After missing the entire 1982 season, Jones reemerged in 1983 with the Single-A Fort Myers Royals of the Florida State League where he made 18 starts. In 1984, Jones was back in Omaha and then all the way back in the big leagues making 12 starts for the Royals.

The only full season Jones spent in the big leagues was 1985, but what a year to be there with the Kansas City Royals. Jones had pitched exclusively out of the bullpen making 32 total appearances, until Dick Howser gave him a start in the final game of the regular season. He pitched the first two innings in what was planned to be a bullpen relay to close the season. The Royals lost 9–3 to the A's at Royals Stadium and Jones took the loss.

The last game of the 1985 regular season was the final big-league game for Mike Jones. Who knows what kind of career he might have had without the accident and injury. But at least Jones finished his time in the big leagues watching his team win the World Series.

Did You Know?—Former Royals first-round draft pick and member of the 1985 World Series Champions Mike Jones was the freshman high school baseball coach for Royals All-Star Billy Butler.

4. Ed "Spanky" Kirkpatrick, Kurt Bevacqua, and Hal McRae.

The American League changed their rules to allow a designated hitter on January 11, 1973 in an 8–4 vote of American League owners—the Royals voted in the minority against implementation of the rule. Although initially approved for a three-year period to start with Opening Day 1973, the rule has been in effect ever since.

The first player to go to the plate in a regular-season major-league game as a designated hitter was Ron Blomberg of the Yankees on April 6, 1973 at Fenway Park in Boston. Red Sox starter Luis Tiant walked Blomberg with the bases loaded to score the first run of the game. Blomberg was 1-for-3 with a single in the game won by the Red Sox 15–5.

The Royals' first designated hitter came later that evening on the West Coast where they opened the season at Anaheim against the Angels. Before the game Richard Nixon made some history when he became the first sitting president of the United States to throw the ceremonial first pitch on Opening Day in a contest held outside of Washington, DC.

The commander-in-chief did the honors before a great pitching matchup between Royals' rookie right-hander Steve Busby (making only his sixth MLB start) and future National Baseball Hall of Famer Nolan Ryan. It was Royals Hall of

Famer Hal McRae's first game as a member of the Royals, and although he became a star as a designated hitter, he started the game in right field batting fifth. Manager Jack McKeon

Ed "Spanky" Kirkpatrick started the opening game of 1973 as the first Royals player to ever occupy the new designated hitter position in Manager Jack McKeon's lineup. Kirkpatrick was a member of the inaugural 1969 club and played for the Royals through the 1973 season.

installed Ed Kirkpatrick as the first Royals designated hitter, hitting sixth right behind McRae.

The Royals took the field for the first time ever wearing their soon-to-be-iconic powder blue uniforms. As expected, the game was a tight pitching duel. Busby surrendered a lead-off home run to Frank Robinson in the bottom of the second inning and the Angels added two more runs in the third. The Royals rallied with two runs in the top of the eighth inning, but came up one run short. None of the Royals' six hits came from the DH spot as Kirkpatrick went 0-for-3 with a walk.

The first hit for a Royals DH came the following night, but again it did not come from McRae. The Royals DH was Kurt Bevacqua, batting ninth in Royals manager Jack McKeon's starting lineup. He had a big night, going 2-for-4 with a walk, three runs scored, and an RBI. Bevacqua led off the top of the third with an infield single off Angels starter Clyde Wright and scored the first run of the game. He also had an RBI single in the fourth off Wright, scoring Paul Schaal. Hal McRae registered his first hit and RBI for the Royals with a two-out eighth-inning double that drove in two runs. The Royals won the game 12-5 behind a complete-game effort by Wayne Simpson, who was the other player acquired from Cincinnati in the trade that had brought McRae to Kansas City.

The first home run by a Royals DH came on Sunday April 15, 1973 in a 12–5 win at Comiskey Park in Chicago. This time it was from *the* Royals DH, Hal McRae, making his first-ever appearance in the position. McKeon had McRae in the five spot in his batting order and it worked perfectly. Fred Patek led off the game with a home run; then after a two-out walk to John Mayberry, McRae's first-ever plate appearance in the role to which he will be forever linked resulted in his first Royals home run—the first ever by a Royals DH.

5. Dane Iorg.

If you are a true baseball fan—*and if you are reading this, congratulations, you are*—you know that every player drafted by an organization does not sign. Over the years that simple fact can result in some interesting connections, some could have been or just missed opportunities, and a few outright oddities. Dane Iorg is one such instance from the Royals' first draft class in 1968.

The Royals, along with their 1969 MLB expansion team brethren, were allowed to take part in the 1968 June free agent draft beginning in the fourth round. But the interesting connection came in the 16th round when the Royals selected a shortstop from Arcata High School in California by the name of Dane Charles Iorg. Yes that Dane Iorg, how many could there be?

As you've probably surmised, Dane Iorg did not sign with the Royals, but they were the first MLB club to draft him. He would go on to a standout college career at Brigham Young University where he was a First-Team All-American in 1971 and led the Cougars to an appearance in the College World Series. He was the Phillies' first-round pick in the 1971 June draft (Secondary Phase), and he signed and began his professional career in the Philadelphia organization.

He was traded to the St. Louis Cardinals on June 15, 1977 and would be a key player for their 1982 world championship team. Iorg earned MVP consideration in that Fall Classic hitting .529 (9-for-17) with four doubles—the award would go to former Royals catcher Darrell Porter.

It would be nearly 16 years after he was originally drafted by Kansas City that Dane first donned the Royals uniform. He was actually purchased by the Royals from the St. Louis Cardinals on May 10, 1984. Whatever the cost was, I'm going to say it was a bargain at twice the price.

He will forever have one of the most consequential and memorable hits in Royals history. Facing off against his former team, Iorg had the walkoff pinch-hit two-RBI single in Game 6 of the 1985 World Series that got the Royals even at three games each and sent the series to a seventh and deciding game.

6. Buck Martinez.

John Albert "Buck" Martinez was originally drafted by the Philadelphia Phillies with their second-round selection in the 1967 January draft out of California State University at Sacramento. The Houston Astros took him in the 1968 Rule Five draft from the Phillies. Then he found his way to the Royals in a trade with the Astros on December 16, 1968.

The 20-year-old catcher began the 1969 season with the Royals' Florida Instructional League club playing only a handful of games. He was called up to Kansas City and made his major-league debut on June 18, 1969 in game one of a double-header, appearing as a pinch-hitter for catcher Ellie Rodriguez. Martinez's pinch-hit at-bat came with two outs in the bottom of the ninth inning—he flew out for the final out in a 16–4 loss to Oakland at Municipal Stadium.

Buck played 72 games for the 1969 Royals, hitting .229 with four home runs and 23 RBIs. He remained with the Royals through the 1977 season. He was the only Royals player from that first 1969 season to appear in the postseason with the Royals. Martinez played in all five games of the 1976

Buck Martinez was the youngest Royals player to appear on the inaugural 1969 team when he debuted on June 18. He was 20 years and 223 days old.

ALCS, hitting .333 (5-for-15) with four RBIs. Three of those hits were in the fifth and deciding game, the game in which he signaled to Mark Littell the fateful pitch that Chris Chambliss hit for his walkoff pennant-winning home run.

Buck Martinez and owner Ewing Kauffman in the Royals locker room in 1976. Martinez was the only player from the original 1969 Royals to be a part of the club's first postseason in 1976.

He was a member of the 1977 American League Western Division Champion Royals as well, but did not appear in the postseason that year. Martinez was the last active Royals player from the inaugural 1969 club when he was traded to the St. Louis Cardinals with Mark Littell for reliever Al Hrabosky on December 8, 1977 (he was traded again that day by the Cardinals to the Brewers in exchange for George Frazier).

7. Mark Gubicza.

The Royals selected Mark Steven Gubicza with their second-round selection (34th overall) in the 1981 June draft out of William Penn Charter School in Philadelphia, Pennsylvania. The pick itself belonged to the St. Louis Cardinals, but came to the Royals as compensation when the Cardinals signed Royals free agent catcher Darrell Porter.

Gubicza made a quick climb through the Royals minor-league system, making 11 starts for the 1981 Gulf Coast Rookie League Royals, 11 starts with the Class-A Florida State League Fort Myers Royals in 1982, then 28 starts with the Double-A Southern League Jacksonville Suns in 1983—where he first teamed up with fellow Royals Hall of Famer Bret Saberhagen.

Both Gubicza and Saberhagen made the jump directly from Double-A Jacksonville to the 1984 Kansas City Royals Opening Day roster. Gubicza made his major-league debut on Friday, April 6 against the Twins and National Baseball Hall of Famer Bert Blyleven. It was a tough assignment, but Gubicza held his own, tossing six innings and allowing one run on five hits with a walk and four strikeouts. Unfortunately the Royals were shut out 2–0 and Gubicza took the loss.

The Royals rookie got his first career win on May 12, 1984 against Boston. Frank White led off the bottom of the fourth with a home run that provided all the offense Gubicza needed—although White tossed in another solo home run in the bottom of the eighth. Gubicza surrendered only four hits—all singles—with no walks and three strikeouts and shut out the Red Sox as the Royals won 3–0 at Royals Stadium. He would win 10 games in his rookie season with the 1984 American League Western Division Champion Royals.

During the 1985 regular season, Gubicza went 14-10, registering his 14th win on Friday, October 4, 1985. The 4–2 win over Oakland put the Royals a full two games in front of the second-place California Angels with two games remaining in the season, assuring the Royals of no less than a tie for the 1985 American League Western Division title. They would win the crown outright the following night.

The 1985 Royals had to rally from down three games to one in the American League Championship Series against the Toronto Blue Jays. Danny Jackson saved the Royals in the first elimination game by tossing a 2–0 shutout at Royals Stadium in ALCS Game 5 on October 13, 1985. Two days later it was Mark Gubicza's turn to keep the Royals' season alive, and he did.

In Game 6, the Royals scored one in the first and the Blue Jays tied it up with a tally in the bottom of the inning. The Royals retook the lead with a run in the third and the Blue Jays re-tied the score in the bottom of the inning. George Brett put the Royals back in front with a one-out fifth-inning solo home run. The Royals then added two insurance runs with back-to-back one-out RBI doubles in the sixth from Buddy Biancalana and Lonnie Smith. In what would be his only postseason start for the Royals, Gubicza came away the winner with shutout relief help from Bud Black and Dan Quisenberry. The Royals defeated the Blue Jays 5–3 at Exhibition Stadium in Toronto to even the 1985 ALCS at three games each setting up the decisive seventh game. They would win the pennant the following night.

Mark Gubicza debuted with the Royals in 1984 and won 132 games in a 13-year career in Kansas City. The Royals Hall of Famer's win total ranks third most in franchise history.

Mark would later be a two-time American League All-Star representing the Royals at the 1988 and 1989 Midsummer Classics. He became the fifth Royals pitcher to record a 20-win season when he went 20-8 with a 2.70 ERA and finished third in the 1988 American League Cy Young Award voting.

Gubicza made his final appearance with the Royals on July 5, 1996 at the Metrodome in Minneapolis. He hit future Royals player Chuck Knoblauch to start the bottom of the first inning, but erased him by inducing a ground ball double play off the bat of Rich Becker, then ended the inning retiring future National Baseball Hall of Famer Paul Molitor on a groundout. Unfortunately that grounder by Molitor was a rocket that hit Gubicza in the left leg and broke his tibia. He missed the remainder of the season.

The Royals traded Gubicza, along with pitcher Mike Bovee, to the Anaheim Angels for outfielder/DH Chili Davis on Monday, October 26, 1996. And with his departure the 1985 world champion Royals era came to an end in Kansas City. Gubicza made two starts covering 4 ⅔ innings for the Angels in 1997 in his final two big-league outings.

The big right-hander from Philadelphia was inducted as the 22nd member of the Royals Hall of Fame on Friday, July 21, 2006—the Royals defeated the Angels that night at Kauffman Stadium 8–3. Gubicza went on to a long career in broadcasting with the Angels, but his heart will always be with the Royals, where he was the final on-field link to the 1985 world champions.

8. Municipal Stadium in Kansas City; Metropolitan Stadium in Bloomington, Minnesota; Arlington Stadium in Arlington, Texas; and Tiger Stadium in Detroit, Michigan.

The first stadium the Royals closed out was their own first home at 22nd and Brooklyn in Kansas City. They thought they had said their final goodbyes to Municipal Stadium over a year earlier on Sunday, September 26, 1971. On that afternoon, 12,338 Kansas City fans bid adieu to Municipal Stadium after 48 years when the Royals split a doubleheader against Minnesota, winning the second game 5–3. But the parting was premature as construction delays at what would be named Royals Stadium caused the Royals to return to Municipal Stadium for the 1972 season.

The real final game for the ballpark came on Wednesday, October 4, 1972. Royals Hall of Famer John Mayberry coaxed a fifth-inning two-out walk from Rangers pitcher Rich Hinton— it was Mayberry's 122nd and final walk of the year. The total made him the first Royals player to lead the American League in walks and set a Royals all-time franchise single-season record. Lou Piniella had a two-out single in the bottom of the fifth that plated Steve Hovley and Amos Otis with the final runs scored at the ballpark.

The last hit was a one-out single by Ed Kirkpatrick in the bottom of the eighth inning. The star of the last game was Royals starter Roger Nelson, who tossed a two-hit shutout as the Royals defeated Texas 4–0.

The game marked the end of the ballpark's near half-century of service in Kansas City. It was also the last game for Hall of Famer Bob Lemon as Royals manager and the final on-field game for Hall of Famer Ted Williams, who was managing the Rangers.

The next ballpark the Royals closed out was Metropolitan Stadium in Bloomington, Minnesota—the first home of the Minnesota Twins. The game took place on Wednesday afternoon, September 30, 1981. With the score tied 2–2, Hal McRae singled leading off the top of the fourth inning—then Clint Hurdle put the Royals in front with a two-run home run. It was the final home run hit at "The Met."

The Royals' offense pounded out 16 hits and Larry Gura tossed a complete game four-hitter as the Royals defeated the Twins 5–2. With the win, the Royals officially clinched a playoff spot by assuring themselves a finish no lower than second place in the strike-marred second half of the 1981 season. The winners of each half from each division were set to play a Division Championship Series (or the winner would play the second-half runner-up if the same team won both halves). The only team the Royals were still battling in the second half were the first-half AL West Division–winning Oakland A's.

Three months later the Vikings played their final game at Metropolitan Stadium on Sunday, December 20, 1981—which was also a loss to Kansas City. The Chiefs defeated the Vikings 10–6 with the only touchdown being a third quarter 15-yard TD pass from Steve Fuller to Stan Rome (it was the only touchdown of Rome's brief career).

The third final game for a Major League Baseball ballpark that involved the Royals was also a memorable last game in Royals history, at Arlington Stadium in Arlington, Texas on Sunday, October 3, 1993. On that afternoon the Rangers took a 1–0 lead when a two-out double by Doug Strange scored Manny Lee in the bottom of the sixth inning against Royals Hall of Famer Kevin Appier.

The Royals rallied when Kevin McReynolds doubled with one out in the top of the eighth inning and Greg Gagne followed with a two-run home run to take the lead.

The game's place in Royals history is large because it was the final contest in the Hall of Fame career of George Brett.

Brett was 0-for-3 in the game when he led off against Rangers closer Tom Henke in the top of the ninth inning. Down in the count 1-2, Brett hit a groundball back up the middle for a single—his 3,154th and final career base hit. One batter later Brett scored when Gary Gaetti hit the final home run at Arlington Stadium and scored the ballpark's final run. The Royals defeated the Rangers 4–1.

The fourth ballpark close-out game came on Monday, September 27, 1999 when the Royals were the visiting team for the final contest at historic Tiger Stadium, located at the intersection of Michigan and Trumbull Avenues in Detroit, Michigan. The Royals and Tigers were tied 2–2 into the bottom of the sixth inning when a two-run home run by Karim Garcia put Detroit in front for good.

The Tigers' Robert Fick capped a historic day for Tigers fans when he connected for a grand slam in the bottom of the eighth for what would be the final home run at Tiger Stadium. Tigers closer Todd Jones retired Carlos Beltran on a swinging strikeout to end the history-making run of the ballpark that debuted in 1912 with an 8–2 Tigers victory.

Did You Know?—*The scoreboard from Braves Field in Boston was imported and installed at Kansas City's Muncipal Stadium when the Athletics arrived in 1955 and remained in use during the first four years of Royals history from 1969-1972. Braves Stadium was left vacant after the franchise moved from Boston to Milwaukee for the 1953 season. The scoreboard is gone now, as is Municipal Stadium, but part of Braves Field remains as Nickerson Field, home of soccer and lacrosse teams on the campus of Boston University.*

9. May 26, 1975.

The answer is an official scorer's clerical error on May 26, 1975 that was not identified until many years after George Brett's career had ended and he was already enshrined in Cooperstown. Which play was recorded incorrect is unclear, but it seems it was probably the first run of the game that was the culprit.

The Royals were hosting the Yankees and got the first run of the game in the bottom of the second inning. It started with back-to-back one-out singles by John Mayberry and Cookie Rojas against New York starter Doc Medich. George Brett followed with a groundball to second base that resulted in a 4-6 force out allowing Mayberry to score. Perhaps the play seemed like a potential inning-ending double play that wasn't, which caused the official scorer to not mark the scoresheet with an RBI for Brett.

The Royals trailed 5–1 before they rallied for two runs in the bottom of the eighth inning on a two-out RBI double by Tony Solaita and an RBI single by Amos Otis. Still down 5–3 in the bottom of the ninth, Harmon Killebrew led off with a single. Cookie Rojas bunted for a base hit advancing pinch-runner Rodney Scott to second. George Brett drove in Scott with an RBI single, then a two-out RBI single by Fran Healy scored Rojas to tie the game 5–5.

Frank White gave the Royals the victory with a one-out RBI single scoring Jim Wohlford in the bottom of the 11th inning to defeat the Yankees 6–5 at Royals Stadium. It was the first of eight career walkoff hits for White during his Royals Hall of Fame career.

George Brett was originally credited with one RBI in the game instead of the two he drove home, and the error was not caught for decades. Remember that when you see George

Brett's plaque in Cooperstown. It's ever so slightly wrong, since the RBI number should read 1,596—but the plaque is beautiful nonetheless.

Did You Know?—*National Baseball Hall of Fame third basemen George Brett and Mike Schmidt were selected in consecutive picks in the 1971 June draft. Brett was taken with the fifth pick in the second round (29th overall) by the Royals; the Phillies followed by selecting Mike Schmidt. George had 1,596 RBIs in his career; Schmidt finished with 1,595 RBIs.*

10. 25, 21, and 19.

The first of the three to appear with the Royals was Frank White, who made his major-league debut on Tuesday, June 12, 1973 at Memorial Stadium in Baltimore. White's contract was purchased from Omaha the day before to fill the roster spot of All-Star shortstop Fred Patek, who was placed on the DL with a pulled inner thigh muscle. The Kansas City kid, and future Royals Hall of Fame second baseman, was the first Royals Baseball Academy graduate to reach the big leagues. He entered the game in the bottom of the sixth inning at shortstop replacing Bobby Floyd, who had been lifted for pinch-hitter Steve Hovley.

Instead of his later iconic number 20, White took the field wearing number 19. He grounded out to second baseman Bobby Grich in his first at-bat to end the top of the eighth. Then he had his first fielding chance, retiring Al Bumbry on a groundball for the second out in the bottom of the eighth. Unfortunately a two-run home run by O's catcher Earl Williams gave Baltimore a 5–4 walkoff win.

George Brett made his big-league debut on August 2, 1973 at Comiskey Park in Chicago. Brett's contract was purchased from Omaha that day to fill the roster spot of third baseman

Paul Schaal, who was placed on the DL with a sprained ankle. Manager Jack McKeon immediately put Brett in the starting lineup batting eighth.

Instead of his later iconic number 5, Brett took the field wearing number 25. The Royals scored two runs in the top of the first, which turned out to be enough to get the win. In his first at-bat, Brett lined out to White Sox starting pitcher Stan Bahnsen for the second out in the top of the second. Still facing Bahnsen, Brett singled into left field with one out in the top of the fourth inning to collect his first career base hit. The Royals defeated the White Sox 3–1.

Dick Howser was hired as the seventh full-time manager in Royals history replacing Jim Frey on Monday, August 31, 1981. For Howser, it was a return to the place his big-league playing career began when he debuted with the 1961 Kansas City Athletics. It was also a return to the scene of the game that led to the end of his stint as manager of the New York Yankees the year before. The 1980 Royals had swept Howser's Yankees in the 1980 American League Championship Series.

In Game 2 from that ALCS, the Royals jumped in front early with three third-inning runs, then held on for a 3–2 win. With the tying run at third in the top of the ninth inning, Dan Quisenberry induced a groundball double play from Graig Nettles and the Royals had pushed the Yankees to the edge.

But that game would reverberate in Royals history because of a play at the plate in the top of the eighth. With two outs and Willie Randolph at first, Bob Watson doubled to left field and Yankees third base coach Mike Ferraro waved Randolph around third with the potential tying run. He was out on a great relay from Willie Wilson to George Brett to Darrell Porter ending the inning. Yankee owner George Steinbrenner was not pleased, and demanded that Howser fire his third base coach because of that play. Howser refused and left the Yankees organization that offseason with Steinbrenner saving face by saying his manager was pursuing a "business opportunity" in his home state of Florida. Less than a year later, Howser was managing the Royals (thank you, George Steinbrenner).

But instead of his later iconic number 10, Howser exchanged his first Royals lineup card with home plate umpire Jim Evans wearing number 21. In that first game, the Brewers' Paul Molitor hit a one-out first-inning double, was followed by Cecil Cooper with an RBI double, and then Ben Oglivie launched a two-run home run. The only run for the Royals came on a one-out solo home run in the bottom of the fifth by Frank White. The Royals fell to the Brewers 5–1 at Royals Stadium.

Frank did get Dick Howser his first Royals victory the following night. The Royals second baseman broke up a 1–1 tie with a two-run single in the bottom of the seventh inning. Larry Gura made it an easy night on his new manager by tossing a complete game as the Royals defeated the Brewers 3–1 at Royals Stadium.

11. Jim Rooker.

James Phillip Rooker was acquired by the Royals with their sixth selection in the 1968 Expansion Draft from the New York Yankees. He was originally signed by the Detroit Tigers as an amateur free agent in 1960 and began his minor-league career as an outfielder.

He hit .268 with 10 home runs and 88 RBIs in his first full minor-league season with the Jamestown Tigers of the Class-D New York Penn League in 1961 as an 18-year-old. The next year he hit .281 with 16 home runs and 80 RBIs back in Jamestown; then .272 with 19 home runs and 78 RBIs for the Class-A

Northern League Duluth-Superior Dukes. He could clearly hit, but he also had a good arm and started to pitch more and more.

By 1968, Rooker was almost exclusively a pitcher. He went 14-8 with a 2.61 ERA with the Triple-A International League Toledo Mud Hens and made his major-league debut on June 30, 1968 with the eventual world champion Detroit Tigers. The New York Yankees took note and purchased Rooker from the Tigers on September 30, 1968. He was a Yankee for two weeks, heading to Kansas City in the Expansion Draft on October 15, 1968.

Rooker made his Royals debut on April 27, 1969, then his first start on May 1 against the White Sox at Municipal Stadium—he took a no-decision, but the Royals got a 5–4 win. It was in his sixth career start on Monday, July 7, 1969 against the Twins at Metropolitan Stadium that he made some Royals history at the plate as a hitter.

The Royals took an early lead when Lou Piniella singled with two outs in the top of the first and scored when Bob Oliver followed with an RBI triple. But Rooker surrendered three runs in the bottom of the second when his mound opponent Jim Kaat doubled with the bases loaded. Rooker responded with a one-out solo home run in the top of the third, then added a two-run home run with two outs in the top of the fifth that gave the Royals a 4–3 lead.

Unfortunately a second Twins three-run outburst in the eighth was too much for the Royals to overcome, and the Royals fell to the Twins 6–5. Again Rooker took the loss, and his career record dropped to 0-6. But he was 2-for-3 with two home runs and three RBIs at the plate. The effort made him the first-ever Royals pitcher to hit a home run, and also the first-ever Royals player to post a multi–home run game.

He did finally get that first big-league win in his next start on Saturday, July 12, 1969 at Municipal Stadium. Paul Schaal singled with one out in the bottom of the first inning and Ed Kirkpatrick followed with a two-run home run to put the Royals in front 2–0. The Royals went on to plate seven runs with a 14-hit attack, including a sixth-inning double by Rooker himself. This time he made sure of the win by tossing a three-hit shutout to record his first win in the Royals' 7–0 victory over the White Sox.

12. Al Fitzmorris.

Alan James Fitzmorris was acquired by the Royals with their 40th selection in the 1968 Expansion Draft from the Chicago White Sox. He was signed by the White Sox as an amateur free agent in 1965 and began his minor-league career playing third base for the Rookie Florida Instructional League White Sox.

Over the course of his first two minor-league seasons he played mostly in the outfield. In the 1966 season, Fitzmorris drove in 50 runs over two minor-league stops—with the Class-A Fox Cities Foxes of the Midwest League and the Lynchburg White Sox of the Carolina League. That season he also pitched professionally for the first time, with brief mound appearances with both teams and a stop back with the Florida Instructional League White Sox. His ticket to the big leagues was punched with that switch to the mound.

He was almost exclusively a pitcher in 1967 with the Class-A Appleton Foxes and went 14-8 with a 2.27 ERA. He posted 11 more wins and a 2.73 ERA with Lynchburg in 1968. The expansion Royals took notice and their 40th-round Expansion Draft gamble paid off handsomely.

Fitzmorris made his major-league debut on Monday, September 8, 1969 at the Oakland-Alameda County Coliseum. He relieved Royals starter Jerry Cram, entering the game to start the bottom of the fifth inning with the score tied at 3–3. Fitzmorris tossed three scoreless innings, allowing two hits and registering his first strikeout.

The Royals took the lead on a Lou Piniella RBI sacrifice fly in the top of the eighth and then tacked on three more in the ninth for a 7–3 victory, making Fitzmorris a winner in his big-league debut. He made a little Royals history at the plate the following year.

On Sunday, July 19, 1970 the Royals hosted the Tigers at Municipal Stadium. Fitzmorris relieved Royals starter Dave Morehead in the top of the third and proceeded to pitch 4 ⅔ innings of scoreless four-hit baseball. He came to bat as a right-handed hitter against Tigers starting left-hander Mike Kilkenny in the bottom of the third inning and doubled.

The Royals took a 1–0 lead in the bottom of the fourth inning on an RBI double by Bob Oliver that scored Lou Piniella. Fitzmorris came to bat again in the bottom of the fifth, and as a left-handed hitter singled against Tigers right-hander Bob Reed. He later scored on an RBI single by Amos Otis to put the Royals up 2–0.

Unfortunately the Tigers rallied in the top of the eighth with six runs against Royals reliever Ted Abernathy. The Royals took the 6–4 loss, but Fitzmorris's two hits made him the first switch-hitter in Royals history to record hits from both sides of the plate in the same game.

Did You Know?—*Pitcher Al Fitzmorris came to the Royals in the 1968 Expansion Draft from the Chicago White Sox and left the Royals in the 1976 Expansion Draft to the Toronto Blue Jays.*

13. Kevin Appier.

Robert Kevin Appier was the Royals' first-round selection (ninth overall) in the 1987 June draft out of Antelope Valley College in Lancaster, California. He made a quick rise through the Royals system and reached the big leagues in 1989.

Appier made his major-league debut with the Royals on Sunday afternoon, June 4, 1989 at Anaheim Stadium, just 90 miles from his hometown. He took the loss and summed up his first game this way—"I could have definitely done better, but I think this is the beginning of a long successful career." He was a winner with that thought.

When his career was done, the numbers alone proved him correct. Most notably, Kevin is the Royals' all-time strikeout leader with 1,458. He also ranks among the club's Top 10 in several other career pitching categories, including fourth in wins (115), games started (275) and innings pitched (1843.2); and seventh in ERA (3.49) and shutouts (10). Appier also places 12th in appearances (287) and 10th in complete games (32).

Armed with a 90-mph-plus fastball, good slider, and devastating splitter, Kevin Appier was one of baseball's most underappreciated pitchers of the 1990s. His unique delivery and manner earned him nicknames from "Planet Appier" to "Bulldozer Bob"—but Appier will always be known as one of the Royals' all-time greats.

But he also has a little place in baseball history as the 27th pitcher to ever record four strikeouts in a single inning. He registered the rare quartet of Ks on Tuesday, September 3, 1996 at SkyDome in Toronto. Appier already had four strikeouts when he took the mound for the bottom of the fourth inning. He started by striking out Ed Sprague swinging, then he did the same to Carlos Delgado—but Delgado reached when the third strike was a wild pitch to the screen. No matter, because Appier then got Charlie O'Brien swinging, and Alex Gonzalez swinging to end the inning.

At that point the Royals trailed 2–0, but the offense started to awaken after the four-strikeout inning. Johnny Damon scored Mike Sweeney with an RBI double in the fifth; then Jon Nunnally scored Tom Goodwin with an RBI double to tie the game in the top of the sixth. It was Nunnally to the rescue again in the eighth with a three-run home run to put the Royals in front.

Appier held the Jays scoreless the rest of the way, throwing a complete game and scattering seven hits with two walks and a full dozen strikeouts. It was his third consecutive double-digit strikeout game, and the Royals won 5–2. Kevin Appier is an unusual person. He was an unusual pitcher, and he did unusual things on the mound—but unusual in the best possible way. Appier was truly one of a kind.

14. Danny Jackson.

Danny Lynn Jackson was the Royals' first-round selection (first overall) in the 1982 version of the now defunct January draft (Secondary Phase) out of the University of Oklahoma. Like his fellow sterling Royals pitching prospects of the era, namely Mark Gubicza and Bret Saberhagen, Jackson's ascent from draftee to big leaguer was remarkably fast.

He made his major-league debut the following year on Sunday, September 11, 1983 at the Metrodome in Minneapolis. The game featured a number of firsts, starting with Butch Davis who got the Royals on the scoreboard with his first big-league home run, a two-out solo shot in the top of the second inning that gave the Royals an early 1–0 lead.

Royals right-hander Frank Wills was making his first career start and tossed the first five innings of the game allowing three hits—all singles—with one walk and four strikeouts. But two of those singles and the walk came in the bottom of the fifth and set up the Twins to tie the game on a two-out RBI single by future Royals shortstop Greg Gagne.

Manager Dick Howser went to Danny Jackson to make his major-league debut starting the bottom of the sixth. Tim Teufel was the first batter he faced and he singled, then Jackson walked Gary Ward. After that rough start, Jackson retired the next nine Twins in order including five strikeouts to get the game to the ninth inning still tied 1–1.

In the top of the ninth, Hal McRae singled with two outs and Willie Aikens followed with a two-run home run. Dan Quisenberry threw a scoreless bottom of the ninth to save the first major-league victory for Danny Jackson as he and the Royals won 3–1. It was the start of an important and often overlooked Royals career for Jackson.

The Royals won an MLB record six elimination games in their 1985 postseason run. But none of that could have happened without the first one of those on Sunday afternoon, October 13, 1985. The Royals were trailing the Blue Jays three games to one in the American League Championship Series. There is no question all of Canada (or at least Toronto) was sure the World Series was heading north of the border for the very first time.

But in Game 5 the Royals tried to send the ALCS back north with the World Series still in doubt. Dick Howser gave the baseball to Danny Jackson to keep the Royals' season alive. The Royals scored one in the first when Lonnie Smith doubled, stole third, and came home on a George Brett groundball.

Danny Jackson pitched for the Royals from 1983 to 1987. He won two pivotal postseason Game 5s for the Royals in the 1985 American League Championship Series and the World Series.

In the second Frank White led off with a bunt single, advanced to third on a Steve Balboni hit, and scored on a sacrifice fly by Darryl Motley. As it turned out, that was more than enough offense for Jackson.

He was dominant—throwing a complete-game shutout, scattering eight hits with one walk and six strikeouts. The Royals won 2–0 at Royals Stadium, where the crown scoreboard displayed a simple message at the end of the game—"Good Luck In Toronto—Bring Us Back A World Series." They did.

Only days later on Thursday, October 24, 1985, the Royals found themselves in the same predicament in the World Series. Down three games to one against the Cardinals, the

Royals were facing elimination again in Game 5—this time on the road at Busch Stadium in St. Louis.

Dick Howser went to the script that had worked before by sending Danny Jackson to the mound to try and send the Fall Classic back west on I-70 to Kansas City. Lonnie Smith and Willie Wilson singled to start the game. George Brett advanced Smith with a fly ball out and Frank White drove him in with a groundball. The Royals got the jump early.

The Cardinals came back in the bottom of the first inning with back-to-back two-out doubles from Tommy Herr and Jack Clark to tie the game. It was the Cardinals' only run of the contest. The Royals put three runs on the board in the second inning, high-lighted by a Willie Wilson two-out, two-run triple scoring Buddy Biancalana and Lonnie Smith. Jackson's five-hit complete game with five strikeouts did the rest. The Royals won 6–1 and the vic-tory parade planned for St. Louis became a parade back up I-70 to Kansas City. You probably know what happened after that.

But Jackson didn't just stave off another match point for the Royals; he also made some interesting baseball history in the effort. Cardinals closer Todd Worrell struck out the side in the top of the ninth, retiring Buddy Biancalana, Danny Jackson him-self, and Lonnie Smith; then again in the top of the seventh, retir-ing Willie Wilson, George Brett, and Frank White. The Royals' hurler would one-up Worrell in the bottom of the seventh inning.

Terry Pendleton led off for the Cardinals and Jackson struck him out on three pitches. Tom Nieto was next and Jackson struck him out on three pitches. Then pinch-hitter Bryan Harper came to the plate for Todd Worrell—and Jackson struck him out on three pitches. Jackson had recorded the rare "Immaculate Inning," striking out the side on only nine pitches. He was only the 18th pitcher in baseball history to accomplish the feat, the first Royals pitcher to do it, and the first pitcher to ever turn the trick in World Series play. Ten years later, as a member of the Dodgers, Worrell also achieved the feat, throwing nine pitches—all strikes—for three outs.

15. Jerry Grote and Nori Aoki.

The Royals signed 38-year-old veteran catcher Jerry Grote on April 7, 1981, just three days before the start of the regular season. Grote's major-league debut was on September 21, 1963 with the Houston Colt .45s (later renamed the Astros in 1965). One of his career highlights was his 1969 season as the starting catcher for the World Series Champion Miracle Mets.

Grote's career had ended after the 1978 season when he retired after 16 big-league seasons, until the Royals made him a non-roster invitee to spring training in 1981. Against what seemed like very long odds, he made the team as a third catcher behind starter John Wathan and backup Jamie Quirk.

Grote said he'd be ready when his moment came. He played in 22 games, making a surprising 20 starts, but his season highlight came on Wednesday night, June 3, 1981 against Seattle at Royals Stadium. Going into the bottom of the fourth inning, the Royals trailed the Mariners 5–0 and Grote was 0-for-1 with a groundout. Then everything changed.

Frank White put the Royals on the scoreboard with a two-out RBI triple scoring Amos Otis. After a walk to Clint Hurdle, Grote doubled home both White and Hurdle. The Royals comeback was underway, but Grote was only getting started.

The next inning the Royals exploded for eight runs on six walks and five hits. The rally started with a walk to John Wathan, then after a groundout by George Brett, Willie Aikens walked and Amos Otis followed with an RBI single to get the Royals within one. Lee May's RBI single scoring Aikens tied the game at 5–5. Frank White's RBI double plated Otis and the Royals had a 6–5 lead. They still weren't done.

Clint Hurdle was intentionally walked to load the bases for Jerry Grote, and why not? The last home run by Jerry Grote was nearly half a decade earlier on August 27, 1976—his only grand slam even longer ago on August 15, 1973. But this is baseball; nothing is guaranteed except the unpredictable, and just like that, Grote hit his second career grand slam.

The Royals still were not done as they scored another run after the Grote blast. And Grote wasn't done either, as he added a one-out RBI single in the bottom of the sixth to end the Royals' offensive night. The Royals won 12–9 and Grote became the first player in club history to post seven RBIs in a single game. Seven Royals later tied that record until it was finally surpassed altogether by a nine-RBI game by Mike Moustakas on September 12, 2015.

Grote would play only five more games with the Royals before being released on September 1, 1981. He played two games for the Dodgers that season, then retired again—this time for good. And that grand slam was his final career big league home run, the only one he had in his brief stint with the Royals.

The Royals acquired Norichika Aoki in a trade with the Milwaukee Brewers in exchange for pitcher Will Smith on December 5, 2013. He was in the leadoff spot starting in right field for the Royals on Opening Day March 31, 2014 in Detroit, becoming the first Japanese-born position player in Royals history.

The Royals captured the American League pennant that year, and Aoki was involved in some iconic moments along the way. Remember, it was Aoki who drove in the tying run in the ninth inning of the Wild Card Game that started the Royals, epic eight straight postseason wins for the pennant. And there was the catch he made in Game 1 of the ALDS in Anaheim. I'm still not sure how it happened, but I'm glad it did.

Another signature moment came during the regular season on Tuesday, August 5, 2014 at Chase Field in Phoenix. The Royals took the lead on a three-run home run by Sal Perez with two outs in the top of the third inning. But it was the Royals' eight-run top of the fifth inning that included a couple of history-making moments.

The barrage started with a three-run home run by Billy Butler. Alex Gordon followed with a single to record the 1,000th hit of his Royals career. Gordon would later score on a wild pitch by Diamondbacks pitcher Wade Miley. With two outs and the bases loaded, Nori came up for his second at-bat of the inning. The first was a leadoff groundout; this time he hit a grand slam home run.

The Royals won the game 12–2. There were more highlights to come with Nori and the 2014 Royals, but that grand slam was Aoki's only home run that magical season.

16. Steve Mingori.

The Royals acquired Stephen Bernard "Mingo" Mingori from the Cleveland Indians in exchange for left-handed pitcher Mike Jackson on June 8, 1973. The Royals initially placed Mingori with Triple-A Omaha, where he went 1-0 in five appearances before being recalled by the Royals on July 7, 1973 as the Royals sent down reliever Mark Littell.

Mingori made his Royals debut on Wednesday, July 11, 1973 against the Brewers at County Stadium in Milwaukee, becoming the first player born in Kansas City, Missouri, to play for the Kansas City Royals. He relieved Royals starter Ken Wright, who surrendered seven runs over 2 ⅔ innings.

He tossed 3 ⅓ innings of scoreless relief, but the damage was already done and the Royals lost 8–1.

Mingo's first Royals win came on Tuesday, August 21, 1973 against the Yankees at Royals Stadium. Royals starter Dick Drago was lifted after surrendering three runs in two-thirds of an inning. Again manager Jack McKeon called on Mingori to stop the bleeding and give the Royals a chance to comeback. This time they did.

Mingori tossed the next 4 ⅓ innings, surrendering three hits and one run, while walking two and collecting five strike-outs. The Royals rallied for two runs in the second, and two more in the third to take the lead. The one run Mingori allowed was a Horace Clarke leadoff home run in the top of the fifth inning that briefly retied the game 4–4.

But Amos Otis led off the bottom of the inning with a double and scored on a two-out RBI single by Lou Piniella against Yankees pitcher Lindy McDaniel—the same Lindy McDaniel who would be traded to the Royals by the Yankees in exchange for Piniella a few months later on December 7, 1973. Joe Hoerner held the Yankees scoreless over the last four innings, and the Royals won the game 5–4 with Mingori getting credit for the victory.

Mingori—born February 29, 1944—was also the first-ever "leapling" or Leap Year baby to play for the Royals—although he was later joined by Terrence Long (2005 Royals).

Did You Know?—Kit Pellow was the first player born in Kansas City, Missouri, to hit a home run for the Kansas City Royals. His second-inning blast on August 20, 2002 at SkyDome in Toronto tied the score at 1–1 in an eventual 6–5 Royals 12-inning win. It was Pellow's only home run in his 29 games with the Royals.

Steve Mingori pitched for the Royals from 1973 to 1979. He was the first player to wear a Kansas City Royals uniform who was also born in Kansas City, Missouri.

17. Steve Renko, Steve Jeltz, and Les Walrond from the University of Kansas; Ted Power from Kansas State University; Aaron Crow from the University of Missouri–Columbia.

Steve Renko was signed by the Royals as a major-league free agent on February 8, 1983 after 14 big-league seasons. He was originally drafted by the New York Mets in the 24th round of the inaugural June draft in 1965. He made his major-league debut with the expansion Expos on June 27, 1969 and played eight seasons in Montreal. Renko also pitched for the Chicago Cubs, the Chicago White Sox, the Oakland A's, the Boston Red Sox, and the California Angels.

He played his final season back at home with the Royals, going 6-11 with a 4.30 ERA in 1983. Renko was the first former University of Kansas Jayhawk to play for the Royals. The next Jayhawk to play for the Royals was utility infielder Steve Jeltz in 1990.

Jeltz was originally drafted by the Phillies in the ninth round of the 1980 June draft. He made his major-league debut on July 17, 1983 for the Phillies, who would go on to win the National League pennant that year. He was traded to the Royals in exchange for pitcher Jose de Jesus on March 31, 1990.

Jeltz played 74 games for the 1990 Royals in his final big-league season. He also has the unique distinction of being the only Royals player to have been born in France. Jeltz was born in Paris on May 28, 1959, while his father was serving in the US military. Jeltz holds the MLB record for most games played, at-bats, runs scored, hits, doubles, triples, runs batted in, and walks (basically every position player record) for a player born in France.

The third Jayhawk to play for the Royals was left-handed pitcher Les Walrond. His stay in Kansas City was brief, but he did pitch in seven games for the Royals in 2003. Walrond was originally drafted by the St. Louis Cardinals in the 13th round of the 1998 June draft. The Royals signed him off waivers on

May 29, 2003. He also had short big-league stays with the 2006 Chicago Cubs and the 2008 Philadelphia Phillies.

The first and only Kansas State Wildcat to play for the Royals was right-handed pitcher Ted Power in 1988. He was originally drafted by the Los Angeles Dodgers in the fifth round of the 1976 June draft. Power didn't make his major-league debut until September 9, 1981 with the Dodgers. But from that start he went on to have a 13-year big-league career.

Power was acquired by the Royals in a trade from the Cincinnati Reds along with shortstop Kurt Stillwell in exchange for pitcher Danny Jackson and shortstop Angel Salazar on November 6, 1987. His stay in Kansas City was also brief. Power went 5-6 with a 5.94 ERA in 22 appearances including 12 starts for the 1988 Royals. He did manage to become the ninth pitcher in club history to toss consecutive shutouts when he blanked the Mariners on four hits on June 2, 1988, then shut out the A's on nine hits five days later on June 7, 1988—both at Royals Stadium. He was traded to Detroit for pitcher Mark Lee and catcher Rey Palacios on August 31, 1988.

The first Missouri Tiger to play for the Royals was Aaron Crow. He holds the unique spot of being the first player from the three local schools to both be drafted by, and make his big-league debut for the Royals. Crow was the Royals' first-round selection (12th overall) in the 2009 June draft, but he wasn't selected out of Mizzou—more on that in a moment.

Crow made his major-league debut on Opening Day March 31, 2011, and although the Royals lost 4–2 to the Angels at Kauffman Stadium, it was the beginning of a record-tying start for Crow. In his debut, Crow held the Angels scoreless in his 1 ⅓ innings of work. He would hold his opponents scoreless in each of his first 13 career appearances covering 15 ⅓ innings. The 13 consecutive scoreless appearances to start a career tied the Royals club record held by Bob McClure (1975-76). Crow was selected to the American League All-Star team that season, only the fourth Royals rookie to ever be named an All-Star. He made 254 appearances over his four years with the Royals—all in relief—compiling a 20-11 record with a 3.43 ERA. Crow was traded to the Miami Marlins in exchange for pitcher Brian Flynn on November 28, 2014.

The Royals have drafted five players from the University of Kansas. The first was third baseman Tom Krattli in 1976, the most recent shortstop Kevin Kuntz—son of Royals first base coach Rusty Kuntz—in 2013. The Royals have drafted 12 players from Kansas State University. The first was pitcher Larry Largent in 1968, the most recent first baseman Shane Conlon in 2013 (he did not sign). So far, no Jayhawks or Wildcats drafted by the Royals have made their debuts with the Royals.

The Royals have drafted eight players from the University of Missouri–Columbia. The first was pitcher Thomas Lundgren in 1968 (he did not sign), the most recent pitcher Keaton Steele in 2013 (he did not sign). Although Aaron Crow was the Royals' first-round selection (12th overall) in the 2009 June draft, technically he was not drafted out of the University of Missouri.

Back to that last little wrinkle. Crow had been the first-round selection (ninth overall) of the Washington Nationals in the 2008 June draft out of Mizzou. He did not sign and played the 2008 season with the Fort Worth Cats of the independent American Association. It was from there he was again eligible to be drafted by the Royals in 2009.

18. Four.

The first Cy Young Award winner to pitch for the Royals was Mike McCormick during the 1971 season. McCormick was signed by the Royals on April 15, 1971 after he had been released by the New York Yankees. The 32-year-old was just three years removed from his finest big-league season with the San Francisco Giants in 1967.

He was originally signed as a "bonus baby" before the draft era by the New York Giants on August 31, 1956, and made his big-league debut four days later on September 3, 1956 at age 17. He won double-digit games for the San Francisco Giants in four consecutive seasons from 1958 through 1961. After two years in Baltimore, and two more in Washington, McCormick returned to the Giants in 1967.

It would be the best year of his career as he led the National League with 22 wins and was a runaway choice for the 1967 National League Cy Young Award. He again won double-digit games for the Giants in 1968 and 1969, but never again pitched to the level of his 1967 season. His stay in Kansas City lasted all of four appearances including one start. McCormick was released on June 2, 1971.

The next Cy Young Award winner to pitch for the Royals was Vida Blue in 1982. The Royals acquired Blue from the San Francisco Giants with pitcher Bob Tufts in exchange for pitchers Craig Chamberlain, Atlee Hammaker, and Renie Martin, along with infielder Brad Wellman, on March 30, 1982.

Blue was originally drafted by the Kansas City Athletics in the second round of the 1967 June draft. He made his major-league debut two years later for the Athletics in Oakland on July 20, 1969. Two years after that, he looked like he might become a transcendent star. Blue was 24-8 and led the league with a

1.82 ERA and eight shutouts. He won both the 1971 American League Cy Young Award and Most Valuable Player Award.

Blue pitched well for the 1982 Royals going 13-12 with a 3.78 ERA, but was 0-5 the following year. He was released on August 5, 1983. Blue was implicated in what became known as the "Royals Drug Scandal" later that year. The circumstances ended with Blue and three other Royals serving prison time. Vida did register 18 more big-league wins over two seasons with the Giants in 1985 and 1986 to end his playing career.

The third Cy Young Award winner to play for the Royals was probably the most colorful of the bunch, and he came to Kansas City right after the departure of Vida Blue. Gaylord Perry was originally signed by the San Francisco Giants as an amateur free agent in 1958. He made his major-league debut on April 14, 1962 with the eventual National League Champion Giants.

He won 134 games for the Giants over 10 years in San Francisco before being traded to Cleveland. In his first season with the Indians, Perry led the American League with 24 wins and won the 1972 American League Cy Young Award—barely beating out Wilbur Wood of the White Sox.

The Indians traded Perry to the Rangers during the 1975 season and he remained with Texas through 1977. Texas then sent him back to the National League, trading him to the San Diego Padres on January 25, 1978. At age 39, Perry was outstanding in his first year in San Diego, leading the National League with 21 wins and capturing the 1978 National League Cy Young Award. He was the first pitcher to ever win the award in both leagues.

Perry won his 300th game while pitching for the Seattle Mariners in 1982. The following year he was released by

Seattle on June 27. The Royals signed him a little over a week later on July 6, 1983. The future National Baseball Hall of Famer captured the final four of his 314 career wins with the

Gaylord Perry was the first pitcher to ever win the Cy Young Award in both the American (1972—Cleveland) and National League (1978—San Diego). Perry pitched for the 1983 Royals and recorded the last four of his 314 career wins.

Royals—the last a six-hit shutout of the Rangers in a 5–0 Royals win at Arlington Stadium on September 3, 1983.

Perry had the impeccable timing of being with the Royals on July 24, 1983 at Yankee Stadium to take a supporting role in the great Pine Tar Game that went down in both Royals and baseball history. The spitball legend was only ejected once in his career, but was an umpiring nemesis throughout his playing days. He was right at home amongst the chaos that ensued that afternoon in The Bronx.

The fourth non–Royals Cy Young Award winner to pitch for the Royals was Mark Davis from 1990 to 1992. Originally drafted by the Philadelphia Phillies with their first-round selection (first overall) in the 1979 January draft (Secondary Phase), he made his major-league debut on September 20, 1980 with the, much to a Royals fan's chagrin, eventual world champion Phillies.

Mark first really made his mark with his third major-league team. He was traded to the San Francisco Giants after the 1982 season and had five years moving between the starting rotation and bullpen, primarily becoming a reliever. The Giants traded him to San Diego on July 5, 1987.

He became the Padres closer and an All-Star in 1988; then everything came together for him in 1989. Davis was nearly unhittable for the Padres, going 4-3 with a 1.85 ERA and a league-leading 44 saves. He easily outdistanced Houston's Mike Scott for the 1989 National League Cy Young Award.

His timing was perfect. Davis was a free agent that offseason and signed a four-year $13 million deal with the Kansas City Royals. The American League Cy Young Award winner in 1989 was none other than the Royals' Bret Saberhagen. On Opening Day 1990, the Royals were the first team in history to have both reigning Cy Young Award winners on their pitching staff.

Unfortunately for Davis his stay in Kansas City was primarily a frustrating one, never quite matching the results he had in San Diego. After recording only seven saves in his two and a half years with the Royals, he was traded to the Atlanta Braves for former Royals pitcher Juan Berenguer on July 21, 1992.

As it turned out, Davis wasn't done in Kansas City. He returned to the organization in 2006 as a minor-league pitching instructor. Davis started the 11th year of his second stint in the Royals organization as the pitching coach for the 2016 Surprise Royals of the Arizona League.

Naming the three pitchers to win a Cy Young Award with the Royals is hopefully a much easier task for any true Royals fan. Bret Saberhagen won the honors in 1985 and 1989. He was followed by Kansas City native David Cone in 1994. Zack Greinke was the third, as he was named the American League Cy Young Award winner in 2009.

19. George and Ken Brett; Tony Jr. and Francisco Pena.

Because you are reading this book, I'll assume that George Howard Brett needs no real introduction. However, you might not know as much about Kenneth Alven Brett—known as "Kemer" to his family and friends. Ken Brett was George Brett's older brother, but there's so much more to say than that.

Ken was the oldest of the four Brett brothers, with George being the youngest of the quartet. Ask the Bretts and they'll say that Kemer was the best athlete of the four. Ken was the Red Sox first-round selection (fourth overall) in the 1966 June draft. He made his major-league debut on September 27, 1967, just a week after his 19th birthday.

George and Ken Brett were the first-ever brothers to both play for the Royals. They also had the good fortune to have been teammates on the 1980 and 1981 Royals.

His second big-league appearance came in Game 4 of the 1967 World Series, a mere 11 days later on October 8, 1967. He pitched a scoreless bottom of the eighth in what was a 6–0 win by the Cardinals. He was back on the mound to record the final out in the top of the ninth of Game 7, retiring Tim McCarver on a groundball to first. The Red Sox lost the game 7–2 and the series four games to three, but his two appearances made Ken Brett the youngest pitcher ever in World Series play.

Ken went on to have a long big-league career, making stops with nine additional teams. He played for the Boston Red Sox, Milwaukee Brewers, Philadelphia Phillies, Pittsburgh Pirates, New York Yankees, Chicago White Sox, California Angels, Minnesota Twins, and Los Angeles Dodgers.

Brett was released by the Dodgers at the end of spring training in 1980. While visiting his younger brother in Kansas City during his incredible 1980 season, the Royals felt they might need a left-hander in the bullpen and asked Ken if he was still interested in playing. Of course he was, and the Royals signed him on August 11, 1980.

He was initially assigned to Triple-A Omaha where he made five appearances before being recalled to Kansas City on August 29, 1980—the same day the Royals placed future Royals Hall of Famer Steve Busby on waivers. Ken Brett made his Royals debut on September 1, 1980. He appeared in eight games down the stretch, allowing no runs over 13 ⅓ innings, but was not part of the eventual American League Champion Royals postseason roster. Ken pitched 22 games for the 1981

Ken Brett signed with the Royals as a free agent on August 11, 1980. He was the oldest of the four Brett boys, while his brother George was the youngest.

Royals as well in what turned out to be the final season of his 14-year major-league career.

The other Royals set of brothers did not have the special opportunity to play together, but they both played for the Royals nonetheless. The Royals acquired Tony Pena Jr. on March 27, 2007 from the Atlanta Braves in exchange for pitcher Erik Cordier.

On Opening Day 2007, Pena was the Royals starting shortstop and he had a big day at the plate. He tripled in his first Royals at-bat, the first triple of his major-league career, and scored on an RBI single by Mark Grudzielanek to put the Royals in front 2–1. In the bottom of the eighth, Pena tripled again to score Ross Gload with the Royals' final run in a 7–1 win over the Red Sox at Kauffman Stadium. He became the first MLB player since 1950 to record two triples on Opening Day.

Tony Pena played two and a half seasons with the Royals as a shortstop. He also made one pitching appearance for the Royals on July 21, 2008. He later returned to the minors and tried to make it back to the big leagues as a pitcher, reaching Triple-A with the Royals, the San Francisco Giants, the Boston Red Sox, and the Chicago White Sox. But he never got that second chance in the major leagues.

Tony's younger brother Francisco was originally signed by the New York Mets as an amateur free agent in 2006. He came to the Royals as a minor-league free agent on November 17, 2013. He would make his major-league debut on May 20, 2014—it was his only major-league appearance that season.

Francisco returned to make eight appearances with the Royals in 2015, the final one coming in the final regular-season game of the Royals world championship year. Pena pinch-hit for Alcides Escobar in the top of the eighth inning and singled to record his first major-league hit. The Royals won the game 6–1 over the Twins at Target Field in Minnesota.

Together with their father Tony Sr., who managed the ballclub from 2002 to 2005, Tony Jr. and Francisco also made the Pena family the first in Royals history with three on-field members of the Royals family.

20. Four.

The first Royals walkoff win in the postseason came on Friday night, October 17, 1980 in the first World Series game ever played in Kansas City. Royals Stadium was packed tight with 42,380 fans to see the Royals take on the Phillies in Game 3 of the 1980 World Series—hoping the Royals could rebound from dropping the first two games in Philadelphia. The Royals did just that.

The game was a back and forth battle with each team never mustering more than a single run in any inning. The Royals scored first with a two-out solo home run by George Brett in the bottom of the first inning. It was his first at-bat since leaving Game 2 during the sixth inning with an aggravating (and public) case of hemorrhoids. Brett underwent surgery during the off day and returned to the lineup to hit his lone career World Series home run. George said at the time that "all the problems are behind me now," and indeed they were. The big stage called for a big moment and Brett delivered, again.

The Phillies responded with a Lonnie Smith RBI ground-out in the second. Willie Aikens tripled with one out in the fourth—the first triple of his MLB career—and Hal McRae followed with an RBI single to put the Royals back in front 2–1. The Phillies responded again with a fifth-inning leadoff home run by Mike Schmidt. Amos Otis put Kansas City back in front with a one-out solo home run in the seventh. Then the Phillies fought right back with a Pete Rose two-out RBI single to tie the game 3–3 in the eighth.

U. L. Washington led off the 10th inning with a single, then Willie Wilson walked. But Washington was thrown out trying to steal third, and Frank White struck out. With two outs, Wilson stole second base and the Phillies decided to intentionally walk George Brett.

It was Willie Aikens who delivered the game-winner with an RBI single against Phillies closer Tug McGraw, scoring Wilson for the thrilling 4–3 walkoff win at Royals Stadium. The victory was the first extra-inning postseason win in Royals history, the first walkoff postseason win in Royals history, and the first-ever World Series win in Kansas City baseball history.

The next Royals postseason walkoff came on Saturday, October 26, 1985 in Game 6 of the 1985 World Series against the Cardinals at Royals Stadium. The game that would become known as the "Miracle on I-70" provided one of the most iconic images in all of Royals history.

The inning started with controversy when a missed call at first base allowed Jorge Orta to reach. Steve Balboni was the next hitter, and he got a reprieve when Cardinals first baseman Jack Clark failed to make the play on a catchable foul popup. Balboni took advantage and rifled a groundball single to left, then gave way to pinch-runner Onix Concepcion.

On the next play, Orta would be the only out of the inning when he was forced out at third on a sacrifice bunt attempt by Jim Sundberg. The Royals catcher turned out to be the key runner, and moments later the iconic image. But first, Cardinals closer Todd Worrell's passed ball allowed the Royals runners to move in to scoring position anyway—thank you very much.

Following an intentional walk to pinch-hitter Hal McRae, Dick Howser went to his bench for another pinch-hitter in former Cardinal Dane Iorg. On a 1-0 pitch, Iorg lofted a perfectly placed single to right field driving in Concepcion and Sundberg to give the Royals a 2–1 hair-raising walkoff win. The image of Sundberg's headfirst slide is seared into the memory of every Royals fan who saw it. Pure magic.

The third Royals postseason walkoff is another vivid memory for every Royals fan. The date was Tuesday, September 30, 2014 and the Royals were hosting the Oakland A's in the American League Wild Card Game. It was the Royals' first postseason game since 1985, and that alone was enough to

Jim Sundberg sliding home safely in Game 6 of the 1985 World Series. Sundberg was the walkoff winning run driven home by Dane Iorg on his two-RBI pinch hit. The 2–1 win over St. Louis was the second postseason walkoff win in Royals history (October 26, 1985).

electrify Kauffman Stadium. Then the game started, and the amps went even higher.

The A's took a two-run lead in the top of the first inning on a Brandon Moss home run, and Billy Butler plated the Royals' first run in the bottom of the first with a two-out RBI single. In the third, Lorenzo Cain tied the game with a two-out RBI double and Eric Hosmer put them ahead with an RBI single. Then the sky seemed to fall when the A's plated five runs in the top of the sixth.

To extend the Royals' season into October, they would need to rally back, and they did—but not all at once. They scored three in the bottom of the eighth, and had the tying run at third with only one out but couldn't score again. Josh Willingham pinch-hit leading off the bottom of the ninth for the Royals and singled in what would be the final hit of his career. He made it count.

Jarrod Dyson entered the game as a pinch-runner and went to second on a sacrifice bunt by Alcides Escobar. Dyson then set sail for third. He barely made it, but the steal made all the difference. Nori Aoki followed with a sacrifice fly and the Royals had fought their way back. But it wasn't over.

The Royals missed scoring chances in both the 10th and 11th, only to see the A's take the lead with a run in the top of the 12th inning. They needed yet another comeback. With one out in the bottom of the ninth, Eric Hosmer tripled to left-center to provide the spark.

Christian Colon hit a high hopper to third and Eric Hosmer raced home with the tying run with a headfirst slide. The Royals were even again. With two outs, Colon stole second base and the Royals had the winning run in scoring position for a third straight inning. The third time was the charm.

With a 2-2 count and two outs, Oakland pitcher Jason Hammel tried to make Salvador Perez reach for the ball, which he did. But somehow Salvy got it and grounded the baseball hard past third baseman Josh Donaldson, scoring Christian Colon with the walkoff winning run. The Royals had a 9–8 12-inning win and Royals fans had a memory strong enough for two lifetimes.

The fourth Royals walkoff win was an all-time Major League Baseball record-setter, and it came on Tuesday, October 27, 2015. The Royals were hosting the New York Mets in Game 1 of the 2015 World Series.

The Royals scored first when Alcides Escobar led off the bottom of the first inning with an inside-the-park home run. But the Mets tied the game with a run in the fourth and took the lead with single runs in both the fifth and sixth. The Royals rallied for two in the bottom of the sixth on an Eric Hosmer sacrifice fly and an RBI single by Mike Moustakas.

In the top of the eighth, the Mets plated an unearned run with two outs on an error charged to Eric Hosmer. The Royals were down to their last two outs in the bottom of the ninth with Mets closer Jeurys Familia, who had not blown a save since July 30, on the mound. Then more magic happened. Alex Gordon hit a blast over the wall in center field to get the Royals even once again. Then it turned into the game that wouldn't end.

Until the bottom of the 14th, when Alcides Escobar reached on an error charged to Mets third baseman David Wright. Ben Zobrist followed with a single, and Lorenzo Cain was walked intentionally to load the bases. Eric Hosmer lifted a 2-2 pitch from Bartolo Colon to right fielder Curtis Granderson, allowing Escobar to score the walkoff winning run.

The Royals won 5–4. At 14 innings, it matched the longest game in Fall Classic history, matching Game 2 of the 1916

World Series and Game 3 of the 2005 World Series. At five hours and nine minutes, it was the second-longest game by duration in World Series history with only Game 3 of the 2005 World Series clocking in longer at five hours and 41 minutes. Despite the toll on fans' emotional state, the wait was worth it—and it was only Game 1.

21. Chris Stynes.

The second time the Royals traded Kansas City native David Cone, they sent him to the Toronto Blue Jays in exchange for infielder Tony Medrano, pitcher Dave Sinnes, and infielder Chris Stynes. Of the three players that came to the Royals, only Stynes's would play in the big leagues. He made his major-league debut with the Royals on May 19, 1995.

Stynes played 22 games for the Royals in 1995, then 36 games for the Royals in 1996. His stay may have been short, yet he did make some history during his time in Kansas City. Stynes's most lasting moment came in a Royals loss, but not through any lack of effort on his part.

On Sunday, May 12, 1996 the Royals were in Seattle to take on the Mariners at the Kingdome. Stynes was batting second in manager Bob Boone's order and he got the Royals off to a running start. Quite literally, a running start.

With one out in the top of the first inning, Stynes singled against Mariners starter and future Hall of Famer Randy Johnson. He quickly took off and stole second base. Then after a Bip Roberts fly out, Stynes took off for third and captured his second stolen base of the inning. After Johnson walked Joe Vitiello, manager Bob Boone went to his bag of tricks and called for a double steal. Stynes was safe at home with his third steal of the inning. Yes, he stole second, third, and home in the same inning.

It was only the 47th time in big-league history a player had stolen second, third, and home in the same inning—the first in Royals history. Stynes was the 24th player in American League history to accomplish the feat, and through 2016 the most recent such occurrence in the American League.

Stynes singled again with two outs in the top of the third inning and his presence on base seemed to rattle Randy Johnson a little. Johnson balked Stynes to second, but he was left stranded. He was 3-for-5 in the game and stole a fourth base in the eighth inning. But all of Stynes's running wasn't enough, as the Royals lost the game 8–5. His four stolen bases were one off the Royals club record held by Amos Otis.

Stynes spent the 1997 season with Triple-A Omaha before the Royals traded him to the Cincinnati Reds with outfielder Jon Nunnally in exchange for pitchers Hector Carrasco and Scott Service on July 15, 1997. Stynes went on to play parts of 10 seasons in the big leagues with the Royals, Reds, Red Sox, Cubs, Rockies, and Pirates.

22. Three.

Bo Jackson is the free pass here. If you are a Royals fan and didn't already have that one, then you are reading this book from back to front. Bo is the first number one overall NFL draft pick to come to mind, but he was actually the third drafted by the Royals.

The first was Steve Bartkowski, who the Royals selected in the 33rd round of the 1971 June draft out of Buchser High School in Santa Clara, California. Bartkowski did not sign with the Royals; instead he headed to the University of California–Berkeley where he was an All-American in both football and baseball. The Atlanta Falcons made Bartkowski the first overall pick in the 1975 NFL Draft, ahead of Pro Football Hall of Famers Randy White, who was selected second by the Dallas Cowboys, and Walter Payton, who was selected fourth by the Chicago Bears. Bartkowski was a two-time Pro-Bowl selection during his NFL career with the Falcons and is a member of the College Football Hall of Fame.

Bartkowski wasn't the only "B" selection for the Royals in the 1971 draft. Their first-round pick was pitcher Roy Branch from Beaumont High School in St. Louis, Missouri. Their second-round pick was an 18-year-old shortstop out of El Segundo, California, named George Howard Brett.

The second was noted Kansas City villain John Elway, who the Royals selected in the 18th round of the 1979 June draft out of Granada Hills High School in Granada Hills, California. Elway did not sign with the Royals; instead he headed to Stanford University where he played both football and baseball. But he was an all-time legend on the gridiron. He was an All-American in 1982 and finished second in the Heisman Trophy vote behind Georgia running back Herschel Walker.

Kansas City fans wish it would have ended there. But the Baltimore Colts made Elway the first overall pick in the 1983 NFL Draft, ahead of Eric Dickerson who was selected next by the Los Angeles Rams. The Colts traded Elway to the Denver Broncos, where he would torment Kansas City Chiefs fans for decades to come. He was a two-time Super Bowl Champion, NFL MVP, and member of both the College Football Hall of Fame and the Pro Football Hall of Fame.

Although the Royals could not stop Chiefs fans' nightmare by signing Elway away from football, the Yankees did briefly after drafting and signing him in 1982. Elway played 42 games for the Oneonta Yankees of the Class-A New York Penn

League in 1982, primarily as leverage in his demand that the Colts trade him. In those 42 games, Elway hit .318 (48-for-151) with four home runs and 25 RBIs.

The Royals also drafted another Pro Football Hall of Fame quarterback in that same draft, selecting right-handed pitcher Dan Marino in the fourth round out of Central Catholic High School in Pittsburgh, Pennsylvania. He didn't sign and headed to the University of Pittsburgh. They did sign a key member of the 1985 championship team in the third round, selecting outfielder Pat Sheridan out of Eastern Michigan University in Ypsilanti, Michigan.

Perhaps in another instance of the third time being the charm, the Royals selected Vincent Edward Jackson in the fourth round of the 1986 June baseball draft. This time they got their man.

Royals owners Ewing Kauffman and Avron Fogelman celebrate with Bo Jackson as the 1985 Heisman Trophy winner signs with the Royals on June 20, 1986. Jackson was not the first number one overall NFL draft pick drafted by the Royals.

The Tampa Bay Buccaneers made Jackson the first overall pick in the 1986 NFL Draft, ahead of Tony Casillas who was selected next by the Atlanta Falcons. He signed instead to play baseball for the Royals and (at least temporarily) left football behind.

It seemed like a gambit for increased negotiating leverage, similar to what John Elway had done three years earlier. But this time the story was a little deeper and the Royals had good reason to think that they had a chance to land one of the greatest athletes of the 20th century. And much of the credit goes to the tenacity of a Royals scout named Ken Gonzales.

Without the work of Gonzales, Bo Jackson may have never played professional baseball and almost certainly wouldn't have done so in Kansas City. The scouting job Gonzales did went beyond identifying talent. The astounding athletic ability of Bo Jackson was evident to anyone who ever laid eyes on him.

Gonzales's work was in building a relationship of trust and respect with Bo and his mother. Bo had promised his mother he would go to college and stay all four years—which he did. Most major-league clubs thought they could only sign Bo before the NFL came calling. The Yankees tried when Bo was a high school senior and failed. The Angels tried after Bo's junior year at Auburn and failed. The Royals knew their chance would come after his college career and not before. The commitment of a single scout made all the difference for the Royals.

23. 75th Round.

For Royals fans who have joined us in recent years, the first thought would probably be Jarrod Dyson—and a good thought he would be. The Royals made Jarrod Martel Dyson their 50th-round selection in the 2006 June draft out of Southwest Mississippi Community College in Summit, Mississippi.

But 50 is not 75, and although a good guess, Jarrod Dyson is not the correct answer. The latest round of the draft the Royals have ever used to select a player who made his way to the big leagues came from the club's 1969 draft class, and the player drafted was a standout for the early championship Royals.

The Royals made Alfred Edward Cowens their 75th-round selection in the 1969 June draft out of Centennial High School in Compton, California. Cowens's climb to the big leagues took five seasons, but the last step was a leap. He was the 1973 Double-A Southern League Player of the Year with the Jacksonville Suns, where he hit .289 with 91 runs scored, 16 home runs, and 81 RBIs. Cowens skipped Triple-A altogether, making the 1974 Royals Opening Day roster out of spring training and starting a 13-year big-league career.

Cowens's major-league debut came on Saturday, April 6, 1974 at Royals Stadium against the Minnesota Twins. It was a memorable day for him, but it also was a contest that went down in Royals history. The Royals got things going early and often, scoring seven runs in the bottom of the first, then three more in the bottom of the second to take a 10–0 lead. There was much more to come. They plated six more runs in the bottom of the fifth inning. Cowens entered the game in the Royals' three-run sixth inning.

Royals manager Jack McKeon inserted Cowens as a pinch-hitter for veteran outfielder Vada Pinson with two on and one out in that sixth inning. He smacked a two-run double against former Royals pitcher Tom Burgmeier, scoring Fran Healy and Fred Patek for his first big-league hit and RBI to make the score 18–6. The next inning held a big moment for another Royals great. Frank White led off the bottom of the seventh with his first big-league home run—ironically scoring run number 20 for the Royals in his first game ever wearing number 20 for the Royals.

The Royals defeated the Twins 23–6. The offensive explosion remained the most runs scored in a single game in Royals history for more than 30 years before being bested on September 9, 2004 (Game 1) when the Royals defeated the Tigers 26–5 at Comerica Park in Detroit.

With his appearance, Cowens became the lowest-drafted player to ever make his major-league debut—a record he would hold until Scott Seabol (88th Round—1996) debuted with the Yankees on April 8, 2001. Seabol held the distinction for all of 11 days before Travis Phelps (89th Round—1996) debuted with the Tampa Bay Devil Rays on April 19, 2001.

Cowens's most outstanding year came in 1977 with the American League Western Division Champion Royals. He played in all 162 games for the Royals that season, hitting career bests with a .312 average, 23 home runs, and 112 RBIs. Cowens was the runner-up in the American League Most Valuable Player voting that year, finishing second to Hall of Famer Rod Carew. Cowens was also awarded a Rawlings Gold Glove Award for his outstanding defense.

The Royals traded Cowens to the California Angels with infielder Todd Cruz in exchange for first baseman Willie Aikens, infielder Rance Mulliniks, and pitcher Craig Eaton on December 6, 1979.

In 1969, the draft continued for as many rounds as any team wanted to make a selection. When Cowens was taken in the 75th round in 1969, the fellow expansion Montreal Expos were the only organization still making selections with the

Royals. The Expos stopped in the 76th round, while the Royals continued all alone through the 90th round.

The draft rules have changed over the years, making Cowens's place as the Royals' latest-round draft pick to make his way to the big leagues secure—along with the major-league record held by Travis Phelps. The draft was limited to only 50 rounds beginning in 1996. It was then further shortened to 40 rounds starting in 2012. When the 50th round of the draft was in place from 1996 through 2011, Jarrod Dyson (2006—Royals) and Efren Navarro (2007—Angels) were the only players drafted and signed as 50th-round selections to make it all the way to the big leagues.

24. Whit Merrifield.

For a college baseball player, the quest to reach Omaha is *everything* and all the student-athletes who made it to Johnny Rosenblatt Stadium found the experience was *more* than they ever imagined. Since 1950, Omaha has been the sole home of the NCAA College World Series, and every champion from 1950 to 2010 won the title on the legendary grounds of Johnny Rosenblatt Stadium.

Of course, Johnny Rosenblatt Stadium was also a desired destination for any Royals minor leaguer from 1969 through 2010. The historic ballpark was the home of the Royals Triple-A affiliate Omaha ballclub once known as the Omaha Royals, then briefly the Golden Spikes, then back to Royals.

The last College World Series held at Rosenblatt was the 2010 tournament in which the eight participants were Arizona State, Clemson, Florida, Florida State, Texas Christian, Oklahoma, UCLA, and South Carolina. The final two schools standing for the championship series were UCLA from the Pac-12 and South Carolina of the SEC.

In the best of three series, South Carolina took the first contest by a 7–1 score. The second game on Tuesday, June 29, 2011 was a tight battle that went to extra innings. Scott Wingo (11th round Dodgers—2011) walked to start the bottom of the 11th inning for South Carolina. He moved to second on a passed ball, then moved to third on a sacrifice bunt by Evan Marzilli (eighth round Diamondbacks—2012). Whit Merrifield followed with an RBI single—it was the final College World Series hit at historic Rosenblatt Stadium and it

Whit Merrifield made his major-league debut with the Royals on May 18, 2016. He was the club's ninth-round selection in the 2010 June draft out of the University of South Carolina.

delivered the first National Championship in any sport for the University of South Carolina.

Earlier that month the same Whit Merrifield, or by his full name Whitley David Merrifield, was the Royals' ninth-round selection of the 2010 June draft. *Coincidence?* Maybe so, but it sure seemed a fitting conclusion which tied three of Omaha's great baseball traditions—the College World Series, Rosenblatt Stadium, and the Royals—together for one last thrilling moment.

It was almost as if it had been scripted.

25. Yes.

Jackie Robinson's professional baseball career began in Kansas City. He played shortstop for the Monarchs for much of the 1945 season and did so at his usual high level—enough to make him the West All-Stars starting shortstop at the annual East-West Game played at Comiskey Park in Chicago.

Brooklyn Dodgers president Branch Rickey was at the forefront of progressive baseball executives searching for a player to finally integrate Major League Baseball, and the young Jack Roosevelt Robinson perfectly fit the bill. The college-educated military veteran had both the skills to compete and the character to withstand the scrutiny such a trailblazer was going to undoubtedly encounter.

The Dodgers sent scout Clyde Sukeforth to secretly meet with Robinson in August of 1945 while he was playing for the Monarchs in Chicago. After meeting Robinson in Brooklyn on August 28, Rickey was convinced he had the right man for his bold move. Robinson signed an agreement that day accepting a contract with the Dodgers organization. The signing would be announced to the public on October 23, 1945.

Buck O'Neil, who was serving in the US Navy at Subic Bay in the Philippines in 1945, missed playing with Robinson but recalled rejoicing when he heard the news. The gap that had existed since the last African-American player had appeared in organized baseball in 1889 would finally be closed. O'Neil explained the excitement for all who had worked for that day: "We swam that chasm and built a bridge back across, so that Jackie Robinson and the major leagues could cross it."

And it was Jackie Robinson of the Kansas City Monarchs who finally did cross that bridge. But there is so much more to the story.

The late winter of 1946 was monumental for Jackie Robinson. He married Rachel Isum in Los Angeles on February 10, and then reported to spring training for his first year in the Brooklyn Dodgers organization. He was assigned to Montreal, the Dodgers' top farm club, who trained in Daytona Beach, Florida.

On April 18, 1946, at Jersey City's Roosevelt Stadium, Robinson broke the color barrier in the International League. He made history that day in a Royals uniform—a Montreal Royals uniform. Robinson would go on to lead those Royals to one of the best minor-league seasons ever.

How good were the 1946 Montreal Royals? Baseball historians Bill Weiss and Marshall Wright ranked them among the Top 100 Minor League Clubs of All Time in their 2001 survey. The Royals easily won the regular season with an impressive 100-54 record—18 ½ games in front of the Syracuse Chiefs. After defeating the Chiefs in the playoffs for the International League Championship, the Royals knocked off the American Association Champion Louisville Colonels for the Junior World Series title.

The 27-year-old Robinson was named the International League's MVP after winning the batting title (.349), and leading the league in runs scored (113). Jackie's now seemingly inevitable ascent to breaking Major League Baseball's color barrier became even clearer. The final historic step came on April 15, 1947 when he debuted with the Brooklyn Dodgers at Ebbets Field against the Boston Braves.

But that well-known story is always missing a small chapter—one that will arm you to win a lot of bets. So did Jackie Robinson ever play for the Kansas City Royals? Almost everyone will tell you that the answer is no, and it wasn't even possible because Robinson retired after the 1956 season and the Kansas City Royals didn't begin play until 1969. That is true, but also incorrect.

After Jackie Robinson played for the Kansas City Monarchs in 1945, and before he broke Major League Baseball's color barrier with the Brooklyn Dodgers in 1947, he played for the Kansas City Royals. *You read that correctly, Jackie Robinson played for the Kansas City Royals.*

Now it wasn't the Kansas City Royals we know today, but those of the 1945 California Winter League, which was the first integrated league of the 20th century. The circuit featured teams of major leaguers and Negro Leaguers who gathered on the West Coast to play winter baseball. One of the clubs of Negro Leaguers was managed by Leavenworth, Kansas, native Chet Brewer, himself a former Kansas City Monarchs player. Brewer could not call his team the Monarchs, so instead went with the name Kansas City Royals. Why? No one knows for sure.

And that is where Robinson comes into the picture. After he left the Monarchs in the summer of 1945, and before he